Ronnie O'Sullivan was born in Essex in 1975. A snooker player since the age of seven, he turned professional in 1992 and was crowned world champion in 2001.

Simon Hattenstone is a *Guardian* journalist. He is the author of *Out Of It*. His highest break is twelve.

RONNIE

the autobiography of
RONNIE O'SULLIVAN

with Simon Hattenstone

ORION

For Mum and Dad

An Orion paperback
First published in Great Britain in 2003
by Orion
This paperback edition published in 2004
by Orion Books Ltd,
Orion House, 5 Upper St Martin's Lane,
London WC2H 9EA

Revised edition

A CIP catalogue record for this book is available
from the British Library.

ISBN 0 75285 880 7

Typeset by Selwood Systems, Midsomer Norton

Printed and bound in Great Britain by
Clays Ltd, St Ives plc

CONTENTS

Thanks to

Mum, Dad, Danielle, Jo, Del, Robert, Gary, Angela and Ray, Veronica and Willie, Janet and Martin, Mickey, Simon, and everybody else who has helped and supported me throughout my career.

CHAPTER ONE

Growing Up

Danny, Dickie and Mickey O'Sullivan were three brothers known as the Fighting O'Sullivans. They were famous in their day. Mickey is my granddad. I used to play snooker with Dickie; he was tiny, a bantamweight. I was 10 years old and down the local snooker club with Dad and Dickie. You had to wear a collar after seven o'clock but Dickie had on just a T-shirt. Dad said to me, 'Give him a shirt so he can stay on.' I gave him one of my shirts and it was massive on him. I never met Danny, who died when he was about 60. He was British and European Champion. The three Fighting O'Sullivans. They didn't really make money out of it, but they were well respected by people who admired what they did. That's because the Fighting O'Sullivans took their sport seriously: they weren't villains; they were just good boxers.

I had a close relationship with Dickie, and he was the one I knew best. I have heard a lot of stories about him over the years: how people tried to take a liberty with him because they thought he was a tiny old man and he just steamed in and did them.

Boxing was in the family. The Fighting O'Sullivans

passed their skills on to their sons. All my dad's brothers can hold their hands up. They tried to show me how to hold mine up, too, but I was never into fighting. I hated it. I had to be pushed a long way before I retaliated.

Dad, like Mickey, grew up in Hackney in north-east London. Mum – Maria – and Dad had no money when they got married, even though Mum's family had an ice-cream business in Birmingham. They had about twenty-five ice-cream vans going at once, and even built their own. They discovered that the vans they bought weren't suited to the ice-cream and the way they wanted it to come out, so they built their own from scratch. You'd go into a massive garage, and it would just be full of ice-cream vans.

When Mum was only 16 her parents decided it was time for her to be paired off. She even met the fella. He came over from Sicily, and Mum didn't have a clue what was going on. She was told to get dressed, put her best gear on. She came down the stairs, walked into the living room and there was her husband to be. He was wealthy, owned two hotels, but he wasn't going to be right for Mum. She said that there was no way she was going to go to Sicily to live the life they all lived. Italian Catholic families were strict: you know, 'You don't go out with this one, you don't do this, you don't do that.' She couldn't stand the thought of an arranged marriage, so she did a runner. She loved her family, but she knew she had to get out.

She ended up at Butlin's working as a chalet maid.

She was going out with a lifeguard when Dad first saw her. He'd been working as a chef at the holiday camp and was about to go off back to London, but he fancied her like mad. He left a note under Mum's door saying he was leaving the next day but she should call him. Mum had always wanted to go to London, so she thought she'd take him up on it. She phoned him and came down with her mate. They both stayed over at my dad's and it didn't take him long to make Mum's friend feel unwelcome. He wanted Mum all to himself. Soon enough, Mum's friend left but, unfortunately for Dad, Mum went with her. She finished off the last few weeks of the season at Butlin's, but then came back down, and three weeks later her and Dad were married. She was 17; he was 18. When they had their first kid, me, they were 20 and 21.

Because they had no money when they married, they went to live in Birmingham, which is where I was born. It was cheaper there, and Mum was close to her family, who, unsurprisingly, were slow to take to Dad at first (they love him now, though). Mum and Dad put their name down for a council flat in London and as soon as one came up in Dalston they went back down south. They made ends meet by cleaning cars in a car park: he did the outs, and she did the ins. That was around the back of Wardour Street in Soho – it was an open-air NCP car park, and they worked there with my granddad, who managed the place.

Later we lived at 105 Eton Road in South Ilford

in a terrace house, opposite a massive school called Loxford Park. The house belonged to my dad's dad before we bought it. It was lovely: the wall between the kitchen and the front room had been knocked through to make one big room, and I had my little bedroom upstairs. By then Mum and Dad had started earning quite a bit of money. Mind you, they were working all hours: they both had two jobs going at the same time. Dad had started working in the sex shops. There'd be the odd bit of hassle from the police, but I laugh at that now because it's so minor compared with what happened to Dad later. Mum was working as a waitress in a restaurant. Both of them finished work at about 1 a.m., so they'd come home together.

My earliest memories are of loads of different au pairs who were there to look after me. Whenever I finished school they would take me round to their boyfriends' houses and I would sit there and play with my toys. I rarely saw Mum and Dad for years because they were working non-stop until I was 7 or 8.

When I was in junior school I often stayed with a family who lived around the corner on Richmond Road. The mum and dad looked after me and the three kids, Greg, Michelle and Lisa, were like the older brothers and sisters I never had. I was always jealous of my mates who had older brothers. They seemed to get along better at school because they knew people through their brothers. So Greg became like my older brother. He was a few years older than me, and he was the best swimmer and the best-looking kid in school. He had loads of girlfriends, and it felt so good walking home from school with him, his mate.

At his home we'd have ice-cream and Swiss roll, and I loved being there. But I still missed Mum and Dad. Sometimes Mum would come home early for something and Lisa would take me round to see her for a while, and I'd start bawling my eyes out. 'Mum, I don't want you to go to work,' I used to say to her. 'I just want to stay with you.' I would look at her and think, She's so beautiful, I just don't want her to leave.

'I've got to go, I've got to go, you'll be all right,' she'd say. 'I'll see you soon.'

That used to crack me up. I hated it. We've never really spoken about how I felt when they left me. I would like to speak to Mum about it, but it's just something that has never been talked about. Her philosophy has always been to talk about the present and to move forward. My family feels there's no need to look back. They don't think there's any need for that healing process, but I think that, as in all families, there's a lot of stuff we should talk about.

Especially where Dad is now. Things have changed so much over the past twelve years. When he comes out of prison things will be very different to how he remembers them. I've never really sat down and spoken about that to either of them.

When I was 7 and my little sister Danielle was born, Mum stopped going to work and Dad started coming home at seven or eight in the evening, and we became a family again. Around this time I'd do anything to please my dad. Dad had just got his first shop in Berwick Street and I helped him to kit it out – all the magazines and bits and pieces. Sometimes he'd leave me with my granddad at the car park while he went off to work. I used to clean Dad's XR2i while he was away. I remember spending six or seven hours on it and when I was finished it was always gleaming. I wanted Dad to be so proud of me; I wanted him to be driving us home, looking at the car, thinking, This is the bollocks. But I was more chuffed than he was. I think I expected him to recognise the hours I'd put in, but he never did. He never gave me recognition; he always brought me down to earth.

Once he had one shop he was on his way. Before he knew it he had a handful of shops. He was a good businessman, and was always a few months ahead with his rent. There was nothing illegal in owning a sex shop, but the authorities were always arguing about whether what you sold was legal. Sometimes they'd come in and raid you, confiscate all your stock, and then you'd have to go to court to fight it out. If you won the case, and convinced the judge or jury that what you were selling was softcore, they'd have to give you back all your gear. If you lost, you could end up in jail or at least lose all your stuff and have to start up all over again.

One day Dad was sitting at home waiting for the result of a court case. He'd fallen foul of the Obscene Publications Act, but always insisted he was innocent. It was a big test case. The solicitor and barristers were there in court to represent him, but Dad had stayed away, so sure was he of his innocence. When the phone rang, he told me to answer it and ask his solicitor if it was good or bad news. It was good news.

Dad brought his whole family into the business: he set up shops for his brothers to run, while his dad did the banking. But eventually it was decided to split up the partnership and Dad went on his own again. By now we had moved from Eton Road to the Drive – a nicer area, and a bigger house. We'd been living there a couple of years and Dad had gutted the place. He'd got rid of the woodworm, built a massive extension, and he must have spent a fortune doing it up – it was like a little palace. I loved that house, but it wasn't too long before we outgrew it and moved again. Dad was always ambitious for us in that respect.

I don't see much of my dad's side of the family any more, but I have always been close to his mum, my nan. I love Nanny Iza. She still comes to watch me play in tournaments. I used to spend my summer holidays with her in Hackney and played snooker all day at Chatsworth Road with my cousin Michael, who also became a professional snooker player – though he's never won any tournaments. Michael was a very good player, and a really nice boy, but I think he eventually realised he was never going to be a champion. In the end he became a manager of a snooker club in Witham, near Colchester.

I don't see Mum's side of the family much, either. Work has really cut into the amount of free time I get. Mum's brothers still run the ice-cream vans. My granddad on her side is retired and spends six months of every year in Sicily. They're lovely people and pleased for me. As a kid, the only place we'd go on holiday was Sicily. Every day it was like a family reunion: we'd go to a different house each day and eat pasta. We'd watch my granddad pick grapes to make his own wine. Sometimes he'd take me up to the mountain to look at his lemon trees. It was great.

Mum's family are proud people and she's no exception. She's so tough, like a tiger. She might be quiet, but deep down she's a fighter. She will keep going and won't give in. She's got that old Sicilian mentality: if she hasn't got a job she'll scrub toilets for a living. When we lived on the fourth floor in our first council flat in Dalston Mum used to scrub out the lifts when her mum and dad came down because they stank of piss. She didn't want her family to think she was living anywhere that smelled. She also never wanted her parents to think she'd married beneath her. Dad says she's just like the wife in *The Sopranos*.

I started playing snooker on a little six-by-three-foot table at my uncle Peter's house when I was about 7. When Dad saw how keen I was, he said, 'Right, as a Christmas present you're going to get a snooker table.'

I did pick it up really quickly and loved it from the off. I used to wear people down with playing:

they got so bored with me and my snooker. Darren, my friend who lived next door, was about four years older than me and I'd go into his house and say, 'Come on, come on, play snooker with me, please, go on.'

'No, I want to paint my cars,' he'd say. He used to like painting little toy cars black.

So I'd either sit there painting his cars black with him or he'd have to come and play snooker with me.

When he agreed to come over I kept him at the table for about four hours. We'd only stop when Dad came in and would say, 'Right you've got to go to bed now.'

That was it – from then on I was playing snooker non-stop.

By the time I was 8, Dad was taking me along with him to the Ambassador's Club in Dean Street in the West End. Dad was working up in Soho in the shops. He'd either drop me off at the club and ask the manager to keep an eye on me for an hour or so, or he'd play with his mate, Steve Godfrey. Dad had never played snooker before I got into it, but then he got the bug and started going to the club. He would play a couple of frames with me, and then I'd sit down and watch him and Steve play a couple. At first the table seemed massive. And it wasn't even a full-size table: it was a ten-footer (full size is twelve-by-six). There were full-size tables in the club, too, but they all looked the same to me – bloody huge. I saw each table like you'd see a bowling green: I couldn't believe how long and green it was, and how fine the cloth was and how big the balls were. It just looked beautiful. I couldn't believe it. I could just about get my head over the table. My arm was always stretched as far as it would go because I was so small. Officially, you weren't even allowed in a snooker club unless you were over 16, and it was only because Dad joined and became a regular in the club at Green Lanes in Ilford that they let me play. Dad and I would go down to the club for four or five hours on Saturdays and Sundays, but he never learned how to play properly. Snooker just wasn't his game: he's got no natural ability for it at all.

I was the youngest kid at the club. Most of the lads there were in their late teens or early twenties. I loved being around adults, and I've always got on with people who are a lot older than me. When I was 10, most of my friends had already left school. The kids in my year were into skateboards and child-ish stuff, and they bored me. I think that might have been why I was so lippy when I was young. I was constantly hanging around adults, and I'd hear them talk and argue back with them. When I was little I could be a pest, and people would get the hump. Eventually I learned that I had to keep my mouth shut – but it took me some time.

At the snooker club I soon discovered that people wouldn't let me get away with my lippiness just because I was younger than them. If I was down there, they expected me to behave like an adult. When I got to 10 or 11, I was told that I couldn't carry on how I'd been behaving. They told me, and my dad, that I had to have respect for the managers who were there, and if I was eating dinner, I couldn't throw my potatoes around – which is what I used to do in the early days. The busiest time of day in the club would be lunchtime, and I'd be there on my school holidays flicking beans and egg around. They'd complain to Dad, quite rightly, that they had a business to run and here was a little kid throwing food over their customers.

I was banned from Pontin's one year. I'd gone down there with Mark King, another snooker player. We used to have a handful of Pontin's festivals each year – one was at Prestatyn, one at Puckpool on the Isle of Wight, another at Hastings, another at Camber Sands. About a thousand snooker players would turn up and we'd play over the course of a week. Dad didn't have the time to go to Pontin's because he had the businesses to look after, so he'd say to Mark King's dad, 'Bill, I'm paying for the chalet, there's your spending money, there's Ronnie's spending money, there's Mark's spending money, just keep an eye on Ronnie. Make sure he behaves himself. If he doesn't, ring me up and I'll have a word with him.'

'Fair enough, no problem,' Bill would say.

So we arrived at this Pontin's at Brean Sands, and Mark and I got to the swimming pool and were dive-bombing. Then we'd try to get into the disco – he'd stand on my shoulders with a huge coat on. Just silly kids' stuff. One day the older kids were urging me on: 'Go on, lob an ashtray,' they said. I was only 10, and so I'd chuck the ashtray and think it was really funny. Not surprisingly, people got the hump.

There was a snooker player there called Fast Eddie because everything he did he did fast. They also called him Sunbed Eddie because he was always working on his tan. He was about 16, a good-looking kid, and he used to pull all the birds. He came up to me and started pushing me. I had a glass of Coke in my hand, so I just looked at him, and threw it all over him. He went mental and chased me all over the holiday camp. I was running between the fruit machines and the Space Invaders, out of the amusement arcade, and through the ballroom where they were playing bingo. I still had the glass in my hand, so I smashed it on the ballroom floor, thinking he'd stop because of the broken glass in his way. I must have thrown it right by an old granny, and she complained, saying that this little kid had thrown a glass at her. I never did; I'd never throw a glass at an old lady. Yes, I may have thrown one at a young player for a laugh but never at anyone I didn't know, not in a million years.

I was reported for it. John Williams, the referee, used to run these Pontin's events and I heard that he was going to kick me out, so I went looking for him. When I found him I asked him if it was true that I'd been banned.

'That's right,' he said.

'But I've not even played in the junior competition,' I said.

'Nope, you're banned. Get off the site.'

I was in tears. I was shitting myself at the thought

of going back home to Dad and telling him I'd been thrown out. So I decided to keep quiet and tell him I'd been beaten in the second round.

'All right? How you doing?' Dad said, when I got home.

'Yeah, I'm all right,' I said.

'Cor! You're back early, ain't you?'

'Yeah, I didn't do no good in the junior. I got beat so I thought I'd come home.'

'Oh, right,' he said.

Two or three hours passed, and my head was spinning. We were having dinner when he said, 'You think I'm some sort of doughnut, don't you? I know why you're home this early – you've been a naughty boy, and you've been thrown off the camp.' That was it. There was hell to pay. I got a slapped arse. He took me to the cleaners.

As a result of the incident, I was banned for one year and made my first appearance at the ripe old age of 10 in the *Sun*.

We appealed against the length of the ban and had to go to Coronet House in Leeds, which was where the governing body for the amateur game was. Some other players were there for ticking off, too, and they'd all brought lawyers to help them out. I just had my dad, but he was brilliant. He stood up and said, 'I don't care if he threw the glass underarm or overarm, we all know he did it and no one's disputing that. All I'm here for is to plead against the severity of the ban.' Dad knew it would break my heart. He knew how fanatical I was about the game. Eventually, they reduced the ban to six months. As you can imagine, it still broke my heart.

I can remember my first century break like it was yesterday – it's the ultimate goal for every kid who's into snooker. I was only 10, the youngest ever to make a century. I came running out and told Dad I'd just made a hundred ... and he went, 'Yeah? Well?' as if it were nothing. So I ran to the manager of the club and told him. He freaked out, and said, 'Right, get the newspapers down here, ring up the snooker magazine.' I was a miniature snooker celebrity. It became big news in the snooker world.

It was the best buzz I ever had. As soon as I got over a hundred, I was so excited that I wanted to miss. It didn't matter what I scored once I got to a hundred; I just wanted to get out there and tell everybody that I'd made a century. In the end, I cleared the table for 117.

Even though Dad wasn't impressed, I trusted him. He had the Midas touch with people. He knew that others could look after me and guide me better than he could in this area. And whoever he picked would excel. He helped out a lot of snooker players who were up-and-coming amateurs or slightly over the hill and in need of a few bob. Dad would say to them, 'Look, here's two hundred quid a week and here's a car, practise when you like, it don't matter to me. Whatever you win, just give me a drink out of it. All I want you to do is take my boy to tournaments and keep an eye on him.'

I remember Tony Puttnam won eight hundred quid and he said to Dad, 'I'll give you half of it,' and Dad said, 'No, I don't want any of your money. Just keep it.' He thought it was a fair deal – they were sharing their experience with me, and I was learning from them all the time.

Although Dad never praised me to my face, I now know that he was dead proud. I've met people who knew my dad and they've told me he said, 'My son is going to be World Snooker Champion.' These people would say to me, 'Yeah, well, everybody thinks their boy is going to be World Champion, but you are. So he must have known what he was on about.' Even Gazza mentioned my dad the first time I met him.

Gazza was my hero, the governor on the pitch, and when I eventually met him we had a good session together. We were at Goodison Park. Rangers were playing Everton in a testimonial, and I'd played in the pre-match celebrity game. Gazza came up to me afterwards and said, 'All right, Ronnie? I met your dad years ago and he was trying to get me to come over to the snooker club. I couldn't make it, but he said to me, "Gazza, you're the bollocks at football, but my son is going to be World Champion at snooker." And I remembered the name because I love snooker. Later I was sitting in my hotel room with Paul Allen one day watching the telly and you came on. I jumped up and said to him, "That's the fucking kid that that fella said was going to be World Champion." '

CHAPTER TWO

On the Road

I won my first tournament when I was 9. It was just a little tournament that we used to play in every week down the club. There were five or six players in every tournament, and you never used to win any money, just a trophy and a voucher that allowed you six hours' free time on a table. I was made up about the free time, even though I didn't need it because Dad always made sure I had my table paid for. But what I really wanted was the trophy, and I didn't get it. I was gutted. They said, 'Sorry, we haven't got a trophy ready, but we're having one made.' And I waited and waited. It must have been about two months; I never thought it was going to come. I kept asking them where it was, and they kept promising that it was coming. One day a group of us were sitting there – it was like a social club with ages ranging from 10 (me, by now) to 25 – and this crappy little trophy was delivered to the club. Nick Terry, the resident professional, told me that when you get a trophy you're supposed to kiss it: 'So give it a kiss,' he said. You're having a laugh, I thought, I ain't fucking kissing that. He said, 'Let me show you how it's done,' and he started kissing it. I've never been one for kissing trophies, I've never had the urge, and I only do it for the snapshots now. But I love picking them up, holding them, touching them and looking at them. I've always been trophy mad.

Trophies have always been more important to me than money. A few years later, when I was 14, I got five hundred quid for winning a tournament in Leeds. Again, they didn't give me a trophy, and I stood there thinking, Where is my trophy? I want something to remember this win by. I'm going to spend the prize money so I want something to put in my trophy cabinet. I came home gutted, on the verge of tears. I didn't even bother telling Mum that I'd won. I just moaned, 'Mum, they never gave me a trophy.'

I may have won my first tournament, but my attitude wasn't improving any. When I was young, I had such a bad temper: I'd be f-ing and blinding whenever I missed a shot – as long as Dad wasn't there. When he came in the club I'd be all goodie-goodie. But people in the club told him about my attitude and my verbals. They'd say, 'You've got to have a word with him. You can't have a little ten-year-old going round the club f-ing and blinding, and smashing his cue on the floor whenever he misses a shot.' He'd come in the club, and if I was laughing and joking when I was playing he'd just give me one look. It would put me on edge straight away. It scared me when I saw that look. He'd never say anything in front of other people, but in the car on the way home he'd say, 'This isn't on. I come in here and see you messing around on that snooker table and I'm paying five quid an hour for you to go in there not to fuck about. If you want to fuck about go round your mates' on your bike. Next time I come into the club, I don't want to know if you're winning or losing. I just want to see a dead-pan look on your face.'

And, of course, he was right. And I listened to him. I had to. If I didn't, and I fell flat on my face, he'd always say to me, 'Well, I did tell you. I'm not right all the time, but ninety-nine times out of a hundred I am, and I don't want you to go through all these pitfalls in life.' He just wanted me to do the right thing: concentrate on my snooker instead of playing cards and the fruit machines, and messing around in general. He always wanted me to take my sport seriously, even when I was 10.

As soon as I started competing in tournaments I realised that my attitude had to improve if I were to have any chance of winning. I had to learn to sit there and concentrate while the other fella was at the table. In snooker, you have to accept that you'll miss balls, and try to avoid showing your opponent that you're wound up because he'll feed off that, which will just wind you up even more. If you start losing your rag when you're playing, in the end you don't know what day it is. Even today my temperament is hardly the best in the world, but it's a thousand times better than it used to be. These days I often come out of a game I've lost so eaten up by it that I say something silly – usually that I'm going to quit. I've learned that only somebody who loves the game as much as I do is going to make those kinds of comments.

When I was a kid, my temperament was only like that in the snooker hall. Outside, I was much more laid back. I used to like kicking a football around with my mates. I was always competitive and never liked losing at any sport – football, table tennis, golf – but nothing used to wind me up like snooker did. I hated the opponent being at the table when I'd missed a ball. I used to get so cheesed off, thinking, I want to be potting balls, not picking them out for this fella.

At school I was quite shy. I was never the centre of attention, and nobody really got to know me. I was especially shy with girls. I didn't have a real girlfriend until I was 15. I'd had opportunities with one or two girls, but I didn't have the bottle to ask them out. I hated school, hated getting up in the morning, putting on my gear and walking there. Because I knew I was going to school to do nothing. I could sit through a lesson and flick through the books, but I never gave it 100 per cent. The only lessons I had any interest in were woodwork and PE. I couldn't wait to get to woodwork, do the drawings and get the saw out. I made a beautiful snooker case; the only problem was that I got my inches mixed up with my centimetres. As I was making it I said to the teacher, 'My case ain't this wide, you know,' and he insisted it was all right because I'd done the drawing to scale. 'No,' I said, 'I've got a case at home, and it's nothing like this.'

'No. You carry on, you've done it right.' Sure enough, it came out like a giant's cue case.

However much I hated school, I never bunked off because I was terrified of what Dad would say. I knew if I didn't go a letter would be sent home, Dad would get the hump, and he'd give me one of those looks followed by a heavy smack on the bum. I wouldn't be able to sit down for a good couple of days afterwards because it would be so sore. I was never grounded, never told to stay in my bedroom. I was just smacked or told I wasn't allowed to play snooker for a couple of weeks. I suppose it was more effective than grounding me because it was stopping me doing the one thing I loved.

I always did my lessons at school, and then got out of there as quick as I could. I ran out of the nearest exit, straight across the busy Redbridge roundabout, instead of going down the subway, to make sure I didn't miss the bus, the 148, which left at 3.24, nine minutes after the bell went. If I missed that bus, I'd have to wait around, and that was unbearable because it would cost me another half-hour at the table. When I got home, I'd throw down my school bag, grab my cue, ring up the cab firm (I can still remember the number!) and he'd be straight round for me. I'd be in the snooker club for 3.50. I started that routine when I was 9.

Dad left me twenty quid every day, which was the cab fare there and back, plus spending money. He said, 'Eat what you like at the club, play as much snooker as you like,' and he paid the bill at the end of every week – which would always be at least a hundred quid. He didn't mind how much I spent as long as I behaved myself.

But I didn't. And in spite of all the money Dad was putting their way, they didn't like me down at the club. For some reason, plenty of people just don't like me. It happens less now, but it still happens. There are always people who want to give me a hard time. I don't know what it is. I find that I connect with certain people, and often they'll be very different from the people Dad connects with. In the past he'd introduce me to people and I'd think, No, thanks, they're not for me. Dad always got on with everyone, and in that respect he's very different to me. I'm basically a quiet person, and it's only when I get to know someone that I open up and can have a laugh with them.

Eventually, when I was 17, soon after winning my first big tournament, I was banned from the club in Ilford for taking in my own food. I used to go to Marks and Spencer to buy my sandwiches and fruit salad because all the food at the club was fried. Monica, the wife of the owner, came up to me and said, 'You're not allowed to bring your own food in here, love.' She always called people 'love', but there was nothing loving about the way she treated me. 'If you want to eat your own food go out of the club and eat it there. Not in here you don't, love.' She was telling me off in front of everybody, really talking down to me.

As she went off tutting, I called out after her,

'Monica, you ain't got a spoon for my yoghurt, have you?'

She flipped, absolutely did her nut. Everybody was laughing, and she went bright red with fury.

That was the end of me at that club. Ron, her husband, came over to me, all stern-faced. 'You can't come up here no more, the way you speak to Monica.' But it was nothing to do with the way I spoke to Monica. I wasn't nasty to her. It was simply that she loved Ken Doherty.

I'd played at that club in Ilford since I was 9 years of age and was their best punter. Well, my dad was anyway. He'd go in there, there'd be twenty people, and he'd buy everyone something to eat and a cup of tea. He kept the place buzzing. Ken had only recently come over from Ireland a year earlier, but the place was full of banners celebrating all things Ken – well done for winning this, well done for winning that. When I won the UK Championship, which is the second-biggest tournament in the world, and Ken won the Regal Welsh, which is not nearly as prestigious, it was plastered all over the club, 'Ken Doherty, Regal Welsh Champion', on beautiful paper in classy printed letters. For me, they put a scrap of paper on the wall scribbled in pen, 'Congratulations Ronnie O'Sullivan, youngest ever winner of the UK Championship'. Ken would also get free time, but they wouldn't give me five minutes until I had my own match table put in.

By the time they chucked me out, I'd had my own four-grand match table fitted in there. I said to Ron and Monica, 'Fair enough, but I'm taking my table.'

'No, you can leave the table there,' said Ron.

'You're having a fucking laugh, aren't you?' I said. 'The table fitters will be down next week and they'll take it away. No problem. Sweet, thanks, Ron,' and that was the end of that.

When I was growing up and people were saying that I could be a snooker champion I never thought about the money I could win; I just wanted to be on the telly. I wanted to be famous, to be recognised. I wanted to walk down the street and for people to shout, 'Oh look, there's that snooker player,' and come up to me and shake my hand. I used to dream of a time when I left school and would be able to go into a nightclub and a girl would recognise me and come and talk to me and say, 'Oh you're that Ronnie O'Sullivan,' and we'd get chatting away, and before I knew it, it would be, 'What are you doing tomorrow night? We'll go out for dinner!' 'Oh, yeah, sweet!' I wanted a situation where I didn't have to make the first move and talk bollocks. That's why I wanted to be famous – because I wasn't very good at interacting with people, and I thought it would make life easier.

I was a funny mix: big for a 10-year-old and reasonably tough, but also a soft touch. I played football for the school and they'd pick on me because I was a little overweight and couldn't do any press-ups. They called me Fatty and laughed in my face, and I'd run out of the school hall in tears. By this time we'd moved from North Ilford to South Ilford, but I was still at the same school, just opposite our old house in Eton Road. I'd run straight out of the school into our old house, which was now owned by a friend of Dad's. I couldn't stand it any more. Dad eventually had to talk to the football manager and ask him why his little boy was coming home crying his eyes out.

I wasn't unpopular at school, but I wouldn't say I was popular either. I had one really close friend, my mate George Palacaros, who I still see now, and play football with. He works with computers and has set up a football website called soccertutor.com. He wants to do one with me called snookertutor.com, which would look at the different techniques used in playing snooker, different things to practise on a table, how to warm up, everything. I've known George since we were 8. We became friends after having a fight.

I went to Highland School in Ilford, and everyone was talking about who was the hardest kid in the school – me or George, who was also fairly quiet and shy. Kids can be nasty, and the school was cliquey, and I always seemed to be the one who was started on and bitched at. Little cliques were always ganging up on me and even though they bullied me, they also thought I was quite tough. Because when I turned, I *really* turned and went ballistic. One day they said to me, 'George is coming back from Cyprus soon, he'll have a fight with you, he'll do you, he'll bash you up.' Inside I was nervous, but I tried to put it out of my mind.

I'm not a fighter now, and I wasn't much of a fighter then, but I have got a bit of aggression. If I lose my temper I'm physically quite strong. I certainly don't know how to throw a combination, but when I'm wound up I'm a bit of a street fighter. However much I tried to forget about George coming back to school I couldn't get it out of my mind. When he finally returned I looked at him and thought, He's nothing special; he's just a quiet little kid. Soon after we were barging each other coming in from the playground, and that's when we ended up having a fight. I threw a punch from somewhere, and he went on the floor. I couldn't believe it. Everybody shouted, 'He's done George! He's *done* George!' I got some respect for that. People looked at me differently. From then on, nobody messed with me at Highland School.

When I went on to senior school I got some grief there, too. My reputation from junior school went ahead of me. After the fight with George, I became known as the toughest kid at Highland. I wasn't a bully, but I used to like Bruce Lee films and I'd practise my martial arts on the other kids. Even though I hated real fighting, if people wanted to have a go at me, I wasn't going to let them walk all over me. I had to stand my ground to stop me being trodden on. I was nervous as hell when it happened, but I knew I couldn't back down. Most of the time, it all came to nothing, but I ended up having four fights at senior school. One every year.

One fight was with an Indian kid who splattered my nose. I didn't know what I'd done to deserve it.

He was a year older than me, and he said I'd barged into him, but it was the first I knew about it. Word got back to me that he wanted to have a fight with me at playtime. I was walking through his playground, which was for the third and fourth years, to my playground when things came to a head. A group of kids was marching towards me, and he was in the middle. I knew what it was about, but I pretended that I didn't. 'Please let me get out of this,' I prayed to myself. He walked up and started pushing me. We had a fight, he smashed my nose up, which was bleeding everywhere. The teachers became involved, but now that I had blood all over my shirt I didn't want to stop. I didn't care: as I'd taken one on the nose, I may as well go the distance. But he didn't want to know any more: he'd got the first dig in and he was happy with that. But I wasn't: I ended up getting the better of him.

I went home and Mum said, 'What's the matter with your nose?'

It's still bent to one side now. He didn't break it, but he gave it a good dent.

I wasn't a good lad. By now Dad was making a lot of money from the sex shops, and there was always cash left around the house. I started to nick a fiver out of my dad's wage packets every other day to go and buy my football stickers. I had two boxes of these little football stickers – they were ten pence a packet. I used to take them to school and do swaps. You'd have to buy a box to get the one player who was very rare. So I thought, If I buy the box, I'm bound to get him, and probably a couple of times over, and no one else will have him, so I'll be able to swap about fifty stickers for the ones I won't need. I've always had a bit of a business head, and at school I was always doing deals.

Dad noticed the money was missing soon enough because one of the workers would ring up and say, 'Ron, I'm a fiver out of my wages.' This kept happening for about a month, and he thought, There's no way I can be a fiver out every time. He kept counting and recounting, and initially thought he was going mad. Then he got a phone call from school. I'd been caught with two big boxes of football stickers, and they'd asked me where I'd got the money for them. When Dad came down to the school he said, 'You've been taking it out of my wage packets, haven't you?' I 'fessed up. 'You thieving little bastard,' he said once we were out of the head's office. I got a good hiding for that: he hit me with a slipper and I was left with a right sore bum. I never nicked anything from him again. Mind you, I got to keep the football stickers.

I was taking my snooker more and more seriously. The first time I won decent money, I was 11 and it was an under-16s competition. I went into school on the Monday and told my mates that I'd won £450. One of the teachers found out and said, 'What do you mean you've just won four hundred and fifty quid?' Then the headmaster came up to me and said, 'Ronnie, is it true that you've just won four hundred and fifty pounds in a snooker tournament?'

'Yeah,' I said. I was so proud of myself.

'Can you please bring in the cheque and trophy to show me?'

Back at home I said, 'Mum, can I take the cheque in to show my headmaster?'

'Course you can,' she said.

So I got my trophy and my cheque, put it in my little bag, told myself I couldn't lose it, got to school and took my rucksack everywhere I went with me – I wasn't going to leave it in the locker. I got a call in one of my lessons. 'Can Ronnie go and see the headmaster, please?' So I got the whole afternoon off lessons and had a cup of tea in the headmaster's office with his mate.

'Can you please show my friend the cheque and trophy, Ronnie? Is it OK if he takes a look?' Mr Challon, the headmaster, was brilliant, but some of the teachers at school had always laughed at my dreams. They used to say to other kids, 'You're like that Ronnie O'Sullivan, you think you're going to be a big star. Well, he isn't going to be anything.' Of course, all the kids used to come back and tell me what the teachers had said. I used to tell them all that I was going to be World Champion, and school was just a waste of my time. The teachers would have a go at me because I wasn't the cleverest of kids academically, but now I could say, 'See? I have done something.' Pretty soon I could say, 'Look, I earn more money now than you do, and I'm only twelve, so don't tell me what to do.'

I started travelling round the country with my mate Robert Chapman when I was 12, and soon enough I was earning as much as my teachers. I gave my winnings to Dad and he gave me enough back to let me play where and when I wanted. He also built me a snooker room, which cost him twenty thousand pounds. It was a huge, 35-by-25-foot room at the bottom of the garden. I had my own toilet, telly, settee. It was like my own mini-house and was where Robert and I did our practice.

Robert and I had first teamed up to go to Hastings when I was 10 and Dad had asked him to keep an eye on me. He and his mates tried to set me up with my first girlfriend, Pippa. She was stunning, really gorgeous, and an older woman. She was 11! Pippa was being all flirty, and I was so shy. She was only six months older than me, but she was so forward, and it just did for me. I couldn't even look at her and kept running away. But from a distance I was looking at her and thinking she was beautiful. I never had the bottle even to go near her. When she was in my vision I got butterflies.

Robert is about seven years older than me. He had a good career with a bank, and even though he turned professional he concentrated on his day job. He used to come round to my house four or five times a week after work about 7 p.m., and we'd practise for a couple of hours, only taking a break for the dinner Mum would cook for us every night. Then on Saturdays and Sundays we'd head up the motorway to, say, Leeds, stay in a lovely hotel, play a competition there, then drive down to, say, Leicester, and do a competition on the Sunday. We'd stay overnight at the Holiday Inn, all paid for by Dad. We used to have a great time: a couple of hundred quid in our pocket, petrol money, food money and speeding up the motorway. I knew every service station on the M1. We had our favourites and used to pick our stations, get ourselves a good feed, and it was such a buzz. We were like brothers and couldn't wait for the weekends to come. He always had a lovely car, brand new every year, an RS Turbo or an XR3i, and it would have all the little gadgets on it, and we'd be flying up the M1, thinking, This is the life.

I'm still close to Robert, and his parents are Mum's best friends. They are the only people she classes as proper friends since Dad went away. There have been a lot of people we'd had around us who weren't as solid, but the Chapmans are like family.

Robert and I went everywhere – Yorkshire, Bury St Edmunds, Stevenage, Birmingham, Wales, Bristol, you name it. If there was a competition we'd be there. We used to look through the snooker magazines and plan out all our dates. I'd have a big calendar in the snooker room at home and we'd ink in all the upcoming Pro-Am tournament dates for the whole year. So when we were practising we always had our eyes on the next big one.

The night before a tournament I'd get out my cue and valet it like you would a car. I'd apply talcum powder to the cue because the conditions were often so sticky that you'd be in there and your cue wouldn't slide through your hands. I'd spend an age cleaning the cue with water and a damp towel, get all the shit off it and then leave it to dry. It was a ritual of mine for every Pro-Am. From Monday to Friday I'd let it get really dirty, then on Friday night I'd buff it for all it was worth.

We'd normally get to a tournament for 9.30 a.m., have our bacon sandwich and walk in. The room would be packed and you could barely move. I'd wiggle my way to the front desk and tell the girl at the reception, 'I'm here, my name is Ronnie, and here's my entrance money.' It was usually between ten and fifteen quid, but occasionally twenty, depending on the number of entries. Sometimes they'd close the entry at 64, sometimes at 128: sometimes, if the club was big enough, they'd have 180 players. At some tournaments they'd say the first 64 entrants are in, so you could turn up at 9 a.m., miss the first 64 and be a reserve. But because Robert was so organised, and we had the big calendar on the wall, we never ended up on the reserve list.

My cue case was bigger than me, and I'd stand there among all these players, always nervous. I was about five foot four then. I could see over the table, but I had to be good with a rest at that height. I think that's why I'm good with a rest today, because I needed to use it so often.

The tables we played on were often well ropy. There would be holes in the cloth and the baize underneath the cushions would be torn. You'd hit a ball in the middle pocket at medium pace and it would jump straight out. You'd just look at it and think, Well, I can't slam a blue in there because it's not going to have it. Then if you tried to roll it in gently it would veer off line. That was amateur snooker, and you'd have to adapt.

My breakthrough came in a Pro-Am at Stevenage when I was 14. I'd never got as far as the quarter-finals before then. I'd reached the last 16, winning two or three matches, and then being drawn against a good player. I just kept falling short and it was so frustrating. I thought, I'm never going to be able to beat these players. At that time I never believed I had time on my side. I thought I should already be as good as Stephen Hendry or Jimmy White. But at Stevenage here I was still in the competition at seven at night whereas normally I'd be back home by two in the afternoon practising with Robert. In the quarter-final I had to play Marcel Gavreau in a best-of-five match. He was ranked number thirty-four in the world at the time, and I'd watched him on the TV beforehand and thought, God, I can't beat this fella, he's immense. He went 1–0 up with a 138 break, but I drew level with a 90, and won the next with a 130 to go 2–1 up. He came back with a 70, but then I had 120 in the last frame. I was so nervous, so tense, but I had never played better in my life. I came off the table and couldn't believe it. Even today, having won the World Championship, I don't think I've ever felt as good as I did when I came off that table. Everything came together – my safety, my long potting, my scoring. I felt like the governor.

He was irate after the match. He wasn't angry with me, just with himself. He had no reason to be, but he couldn't believe he had played so well and been beaten by a 14-year-old. He came off the table saying, 'Gee, that kid, he's unbelievable, where's he come from? Nobody's ever played that well against me.' I was so chuffed.

My reputation was growing by the minute. It had gone round the room that Ronnie O'Sullivan had just beaten Marcel Gavreau. There were probably about thirty people there to watch – locals who played in the club every week and those who would drop in if there was a Pro-Am on. Professionals like Dean O'Kane would turn up and people would turn out to see them. You got a grand for winning a Pro-Am, which was a lot of money for them so they used to nick a few quid, and it was good match practice as well.

In the semi-final I played like shit but still blitzed my opponent 3–1. I couldn't play as well as I had against Gavreau, but I got through, which was the important thing. I'd been beaten in the last 32 of tournaments when playing better than I did in the semi, but here I was through to a final. I had to wait a couple of hours because the other semi was still being played. Anthony Hamilton was in it, and I was sure he'd win so I'd be up against him in the final, but I didn't care. I'd got to the final, and I knew my face was going to be in the snooker magazine. I couldn't wait to see it. The magazine had the professional section at the beginning, and the last few pages were dedicated to the amateurs and the women. I'd be able to go down the snooker club, show the magazine around, and all the regulars would think, Fuck me, Ronnie got to the final.

I beat Anthony Hamilton 3–2 in the final. It was about midnight when we started the match, and we finished about 1.30 a.m. I was 2–1 down and it was a black-ball frame. The scores were tied, so we respotted the black and I won the toss. He played a good safety shot and left me a double. I just thought, Whatever will be will be. I wasn't playing that well, and as I said I didn't really care because I'd already achieved more than enough by getting through to the final. So I gave it a crack and it sank so sweetly into the middle of the pocket.

Robert was sitting watching. He isn't the most excitable of men, but he did look pretty thrilled. He knew I was one frame away from winning the biggest Pro-Am on the circuit. One hundred and eighty players had started the tournament at Stevenage, and now it was me against one other player in the last frame of the last match.

I won the final frame quite easily – 61–30, I think. Anthony shook my hand, and I was thinking, I've just won a thousand quid. I'm 14 years old and I'm just about to be given a cheque for a grand, and I'm going to have a mega write-up and everybody's going to read about it. Winning a final at 14 – it was unheard of. I knew that the week after, at the next Pro-Am, everybody would be looking at me. It was going to be such a buzz to walk in, just like when Peter Ebdon and Anthony Hamilton walked into the room at a Pro-Am tournament, and people would shiver and shit themselves. I thought, I've arrived!

As well as travelling with Robert, I used to go around the Pro-Am circuit with a fella called Johnny O'Brien. Dad paid him to chaperone me, about £250 a week, and gave him a car and expenses. All he had to do for it was take me to tournaments at the weekend. Dad was too busy enjoying life to do the job himself. And anyway, I didn't want him to come because it would put too much pressure on me. If I missed a ball, he'd sit there and get the hump, and it took the enjoyment away.

I never told Dad I didn't want him with me any more at matches, but it just worked out that way. Mum and Dad had started going out to a lot to clubs when I was only 12. They felt they'd worked their arses off for years, had finally made themselves some money, and now it was time to enjoy it. Dad especially enjoyed having loads of money and being able to go wherever he wanted. He and Mum would go to Browns, which was a seriously exclusive club, and stay there till seven or eight in the morning. He always went with Mum, but never liked dancing, so he got this gay fella that he knew, Stephen Atwell, who was six foot six, to dance with my mum all night. Dad would just talk and make people laugh. He never drank, but he'd often settle the whole bar bill at the end of the night. He was such a spend-freak. He thought he had to buy everyone drinks and he could afford it. This was the late eighties and his chain of shops was thriving.

The first tournament I went to with Johnny was the British Amateur. I was beaten 4–3 by Mukish Palmer, but I'd won a couple of matches to get to play him, and Mukish was winning amateur tournaments whereas I was ranked only 112th. It was a great achievement for me so I was buzzing when I got back. Dad said to Johnny, 'How's about you and Ronnie being a team?' It was a perfect arrangement for all of us.

At the time there were a lot of good junior snooker players around: Chris Brooks, who was a couple of years older than me and became my doubles partner; Mark King, also two years older than me; and Chris Scanlon, who was the closest to me in ability or, if anything, a bit ahead of me then. But he was more of a hustler. He played in all the midnight fliers at Tottenham when he was 11 and 12, but I wasn't allowed to at that time. He went to live in Holland when he was about 14 because it was easy money for him there – this fella was paying his wages and all he had to do was play in his snooker club. His was a tragic waste of talent. I remember playing him in Amsterdam, and Chris took off his waistcoat, folded it up and put it in his jacket. I thought, What is he doing? But he'd lost the plot: the distractions of Amsterdam had become too much for him. Chris would have been where I am today if he'd had the application, but his game deteriorated. There were times when he was still a great player, and he even made 147s, but he hadn't played against the tough competition that I was playing week in week out. You need to be getting beat and learn how to take it before you can become a real winner.

A midnight flier is a tournament that starts at midnight and finishes about ten in the morning. It's also often called the Graveyard. The few times I played in them I didn't really enjoy it because I'd be half a kip by two in the morning. They used a handicapping system and there was a lot of cheating. I'd give someone a 60 start, and they'd make an 80 break against me. So I'd be thinking, This geeza is better than me. How come I had to give him a 60 start? I used to hate that. There were a lot of ringers – bandits, we used to call them.

The Pro-Am tournaments were slightly handicapped, too, but much fairer. Marcel Gavreau would probably give me a 14 or 7 start in each frame. It doesn't seem much, but it can be vital in a close-scoring game. Even then it could be ridiculous. For example, Willie Thorne may have given Peter Ebdon a 14 start whereas really it was Willie who needed the start. Because he'd played through the clubs, Ebdon was used to playing on poor tables, whereas if it wasn't like a bowling green, Willie would moan like anything. He even moaned about professional conditions. I, on the other hand, loved it because you had to adapt.

Sometimes, the amateurs were simply better than the professionals. For instance, Dean O'Kane would come to Ilford and play Ken Doherty, but Ken was a different class to him. They'd play each other for, say, eight hundred quid, which was a fortune for Ken at the time. So Dad would put £300 in, Ken would put £200 in, and someone else would come up with the rest. Dad used to do a lot of the backing.

At one stage, Brian Morgan, who was a very good player and is now ranked around thirty in the world, was in Basildon when Ken was in Ilford. So there were only twenty miles between them, and the competition was intense. Everyone in Basildon thought Brian was better, and everyone in Ilford *knew* Ken was better. They used to have money matches, and once Brian refused to play for less than a grand. Ken didn't have the money, so Dad said, 'Yeah, I'll put a grand up. Tell Brian you'll play him on any table anywhere.' In the end, the match never happened.

Essex was always an incredibly strong area for snooker. There were Martin Smith, Dave Gilbert, Nick Terry, John Wright, Gary Filtness, Joe Oboy and Tony Puttnam – people you may well not have heard of, but all very good players. Tony Puttnam packed in the game and has worked for Mum in the porno business for the past ten years.

I learned a lot of my snooker from Eugene Hughes. He was based at Ilford and was the top Irish player. So when the Irish lads, like Ken Doherty, came over, they based themselves in Ilford, and Eugene was like a father figure to them. Eamonn Dunphy, the former footballer and writer, who had connections with Eugene, asked him to look after the boys, and he helped them out with money. So Ilford was full of the Irish, while neighbouring Barking, which was a brilliant club, was full of home-grown talent like Nick Terry, Tony Puttnam and Gary Filtness.

I was a member of both Ilford and Barking, so I'd go to one four times and to the other three times each week. That was in addition to the practice I put in on my own table at home. At 14, I'd play six or seven hours a day when I wasn't at school and maybe three or four hours a day when I was. That was my homework. I used to leave the official homework stuff to a kid called Fasel Nadir, who I used to pay to do it. He was brilliant, but I told him not to make it too clever, otherwise they'd know it wasn't mine. Fasel was in my tutor group, so we'd go to registration together and then he'd go off to the top-stream classes and I'd go off to the bottom. I'd give him a fiver to do the homework and I didn't even copy it out after he'd done it: I just collected it off him at registration each morning. He did the business: I got Cs and Ds for his work, which satisfied the teachers and just about satisfied Mum and Dad.

There were a good few players who were strong amateurs and could have been solid professionals, but their attitude was wrong. Nick Terry would have been a good pro if he'd concentrated on snooker, but he was a good-looking lad, started going out with girls, and that was that. He just lost it. But I remember picking balls out for him for seven or eight hours until I had blisters on my feet and couldn't do it any more. It was a good experience, though, something you need to go through. Nowadays I do the same thing to kids. I can't ease up: I want to make a century every time I go to the table. It may be painful at the time, but I'm sure it does them good.

When I was 13 I had a sparring partnership with Ken Doherty, and it was probably one of the toughest, most demoralising things I've been through. I had three days of him in my snooker room at home, and in the end I said to him, 'Ken, I've got to go somewhere.' He said OK, got his cue case and left. He came back half an hour later because he'd forgotten something and I was still in there practising. I'd just had to get him out of the house. I felt ashamed because I was sure he was thinking I'd bottled out of playing him, but I couldn't take any more. And because he was a winner he didn't show me any mercy. He just wanted to win.

Next day I drew him in a competition at Barking. I couldn't believe it – just my luck. But he wasn't there. If you are two minutes late for your match they say, 'Right you're scratched' and a reserve steps in. Half an hour went by and I was thinking, I've had a right touch. Meanwhile, Ken had rung up and said he'd just got out of bed and asked who he'd been drawn against. When they said Ronnie, he said, 'Would he mind if I was a little bit late?' He knew that by rights the match should have been scratched, and said it was fine if I wanted to play the reserve. The organisers came over and asked me, 'Do you want to play him?' In my mind I said, 'No, I don't want to play him; it's the last thing I want to do,' but I said, 'Yeah, I'll play him.' He eventually turned up and they put us on a table. I had chance after chance, but I couldn't take any of them. He played like shit but still hammered me 4–0. I was just scared. I had too much respect for him. Psychologically, he battered me. I treated him as a god instead of just playing the balls. At the time, Ken was World Amateur Champion and World Junior Champion and he was just about to turn professional. He'd only been over from Ireland a year or two and shared a rented house with six or seven other Irish players in Ilford. They used to earn their livings by playing cards at the club and winning Pro-Ams at £1,000 a pop. They are all about six or seven years older than me, and they didn't like me when I was a little kid. I don't think most of them like me much better today, either. I don't know if it was because they thought I was mouthy or flash, or that I had everything. I think they feel that I was lucky because Dad had the money to support me.

A lot of people think that money can make you into a World Champion. People occasionally say, 'It's because your dad had money that you made the grade,' and that if they'd had everything on a plate and could have practised all the hours I practised, then they would have been World Champion too. These people often have a young son who is a footballer or a snooker player. They say that I improved so quickly because I had a snooker table in my house and could practise all the hours I wanted. And fair enough, I'm sure having my own table helped me, but I'm equally sure having your own table doesn't turn you into a World Champion.

On a Monday Ken would play a fella called Mickey Rowatt on his own table in the club. Now Mickey wasn't a good player by any stretch of the imagination but Ken would play him for five or six hours and this fella would just be there picking out balls for him. I was only 14, but I could have given Mickey a 50 start, played him blindfolded and still won. I couldn't understand why Ken – who'd just turned professional – wanted to play him, because he couldn't offer him any competition. I found it frustrating. When he was there playing Mickey, it meant I wouldn't get a game with him all day. I'd have to go and play on one of the tables down the hall or practise on my own. And all I wanted to do was play Ken, or at least play on his good table. The difference in standard between Ken's table and the others was amazing: it was like playing on a carpet rather than an ice-skating rink. The table I usually played on at the club was filthy.

Typically, I'd say to Ken, 'Do you want a game tomorrow?' and he'd say, 'No, I can't, because I'm playing Mickey, but I'll give you a game on Thursday.' So I'd have to wait two or three days for a game. By then I'd have been playing on shit tables for so long that I'd be useless, and it would take an hour or two before I started giving as good as I got. Then I wouldn't get another game for four or five days and I'd go downhill again.

Mickey might have been rubbish but he was a

professional. Anybody could be a professional. All you had to do was pay your £500 subscription fee and £100 at each tournament and that was it – professional. There were plenty of people who thought all they had to do was get on telly once and they'd cracked it. The game was full of people with big delusions.

Day after day I'd sit at the club watching, thinking that any minute Mickey would say, 'I don't want to play any more, Ken, I've had it.' But he was a glutton for punishment. Sometimes he'd finally go home, have a shower, and then come back in the evening all suited and booted with his cue case ready for more humiliation. It meant that I wouldn't get a look-in even in the evenings, and it wound me up.

I know I annoyed Ken. I used to ask him irritating questions. He's got a scar on his face, and one day I asked, 'Ken, how d'you get that scar?' He said, 'Don't be such a nosy little bastard.' It frightened me. I thought I must have upset him and that upset me because, to me, he was a hero. I spent so much time around him, watching him potting balls and fishing them out for him. I thought he was brilliant, and he never seemed to miss, and perhaps if I copied his action I would never miss as well. So I copied every-thing – not only his cue action and his attitude, but even the way he opened his mouth on the shot. But copying Ken was the worst thing that ever happened to my snooker. His hand was very loose and wide open. I copied his action for about three years, but now I know it's a style Ken has made his own and one that doesn't work for me. Today, as a result of copying Ken, I dip into shots instead of going through the cue ball, so I chip over the ball. These are quirks I'm now trying to iron out with my coach. Before I started copying Ken I used to play like Steve Davis: I would bring the cue right back and my arm was straight. I think if I'd stuck with the Nugget's technique and combined it with my exciting game, the chances are I would have won three World Championships by now. Steve Davis was my first great hero, because he won all the time. Today, I watch videos of myself at 14, when my game was modelled on Steve's, and I try to get back to how I was then. It makes me miserable looking at the old videos, though: I've got to move forward now and find a solution rather than dwelling on the problem. That doesn't go just for snooker; it goes for life.

I beat Ken for the first time in competition when I was 13. His attitude towards me changed then. As soon as I started becoming a threat he spoke to me differently – warmer, more respectful: 'How did you get on, Ronnie? Did you win that competition?' He'd say hello to everybody else, but I could feel he had his eye on me, like a big brother, and I loved that. We get on fine these days. He's a nice fella.

After a quiet start at school, I became fairly disruptive. They put all the naughty kids in one class in the third and fourth years, and we used to cause havoc. They'd have to bring in supply teachers regularly because our teachers had had breakdowns or couldn't face teaching us. Then the supply teachers would crack up halfway through a lesson, admitting in front of us that they couldn't handle it. When a teacher threatened to send us to the head for talking, we'd just say, 'Fine,' and carry on talking. It must have been a nightmare for them.

At lunch I used to go down the snooker hall with George and a few other friends – Robert Young, Richard Basham and Chris Johnston – and they would put their dinner money on me. I hate playing with other people's money because I can't stand the thought of them losing their cash. But I never used to lose, even though I had to use a racker – a cue out of the rack. There'd always be a couple of fellas in the club. 'D'you fancy a game?' I'd say. 'I'll give you two quid a frame.' I'd give them a 30 start, and all the kids would put in their fifty pences. After the first frame I'd offer to double up their money, and we'd come out with about a tenner and steam down to the fish and chip shop. We'd stroll back into school with a big bag of fish and chips just in time for afternoon lessons.

All my mates were much more into football than snooker. George was a brilliant footballer and everybody said he'd be playing for West Ham when he was older. I was happy for him but it frustrated me because none of my friends knew anything about snooker and couldn't tell how good I was. If I'd played football at the same level that I played snooker, I would have been the most popular kid in school with the girls. But snooker wasn't that cool.

It wasn't really even thought of as a sport.

I was a right little fucker at school, but somehow I managed to get on well with the teachers who mattered – Mr Challon, the head, and Mrs Abbot, the deputy head. Mrs Abbot loved me – I couldn't do any wrong in her eyes. I went back to see her after I had left and she just opened up her arms and took me in them and shouted, '*Ronnnnie!*'

When I was still at school she wrote Mum and Dad a letter saying how proud they must be of me because I had been on television playing in a tournament called the Cockney Classic. To qualify for that tournament, first you had to win a competition in your local club – you played a single frame against six players. Then the winners from that stage went to another qualifying round in which you had to win another six frames. In that second stage hardly anybody scored a point against me – I had breaks of 70, 60, 80, 90, 70 and 60. So I had qualified for the Cockney Classic. Dad took me out and got me togged up from head to foot: shirt, suit and a waistcoat like Steve Davis's, with no buckle at the back. I thought, I've got to look good for the telly.

The day after it had been on TV I turned up for my cooking lesson at school. Mrs McFee was another tough teacher if you got on the wrong side of her, but we got on great. She used to wear different-coloured contact lenses because she was obsessed with cats. So one day she'd have piercing blue eyes and then the next she'd have green eyes. I used to look in her eyes, and think, *phwoah*! She wasn't beautiful, but there was something attractive about her. Something nice, something sexy. Another teacher, Mrs Hayes, was taking the lesson, too. Mrs Hayes *was* beautiful, and a real softy. She had the patience of a saint. Mrs McFee was the opposite. So if we were playing up towards Mrs Hayes, Mrs McFee would just look over and you'd quickly rein yourself in. It was a 'good cop, bad cop' deal. That day, Mrs McFee said, 'Right, we're not doing any cooking today, we're going to watch a video. We have someone in our class who was on television yesterday.' By this time, I'm thinking, Fucking hell, this is me.

She put on the video, and all the kids were looking at me, wondering how on earth I'd got on telly. They'd probably been in bed by 10 p.m., and this had been on ITV at 11.30 p.m. I was playing Steve Ventham, who was English Amateur Champion, and had been the youngest English under-16 Champion. He was 23 now and winning big events. He played a good safety shot but I still potted the red in the middle and then knocked in 75 – my first break on TV. Steve Davis was commentating, and the Nugget was well impressed. I'd not seen the performance before now and I sat there watching myself on the video, loving it. I was beaten in the semi-finals of the Cockney Classic, but I received a trophy for getting that far. It went round school like a whirlwind that I'd been on telly, and people came up to me and asked, 'Are you going to be a top snooker player?'

That year, when I was 14, I played in an exhibition

against Stephen Hendry. He was being driven around by a fella called John Carroll, who still drives for him today. John works for the snooker manager Ian Doyle, and he does the driving for all his players, and gets their food, pays their hotel bills and deals with the day-to-day problems snooker players face at tournaments. And when they're not at tournaments he's like a friend to them. At this exhibition Dad started speaking to John Carroll in the Gents' and asked him what had brought him down there that night.

'I drive Stephen Hendry about,' said John. 'I'm keeping an eye on a player called Ronnie O'Sullivan.'

'Oh, I'm his dad.'

They got chatting, and it turned out that Ian Doyle wanted to sign me up there and then. But because he knew Dad had a bit of money, he didn't think there was any way I'd sign for him, so they didn't even offer me a contract. I probably would have been offered his standard contract for new players: a sponsored car and all entry fees to tournaments in return for 20 per cent of competition earnings and 20 per cent of off-the-table earnings. Unless you had a couple of appearances on the television show *Big Break* or you played a couple of exhibitions for four hundred pounds a night, this wasn't much money at all. For most players, it would mean you'd have just enough to live on. Then it's down to you to get a few results, and that's when Ian Doyle would start setting up sponsorship deals and managing the player's day-to-day business affairs. But he didn't think I'd need all that because Dad was in a financially secure position, so he backed off.

That night Stephen Hendry, who had just won the World Championship, played Alison Fisher, the Women's World Champion, best of five, and one frame against each of six local amateurs. When I played him, he had a 40 break and then I matched it. It went down to the last red and I could have played safe and snookered him. Dad shouted out from the crowd, 'Go for the double,' and I did. I didn't really want to play such a risky shot because I desperately wanted to beat the World Champion. But I thought, Stephen Hendry is the star of the show and I'm just a little kid playing him, and if Dad thought it was right to go for the double then that was the way to do it. So I went for the double, missed and he cleared the table.

At that stage I usually did what Dad said, and I realise now that there was a principle behind what he'd said. Stephen Hendry was World Champion, I was 14 years old, and Dad didn't want me going out and tucking him up. He just wanted me to enjoy the game and go for the shots out of respect to Stephen. He didn't say anything that night, but deep down I knew he was proud to see me playing Stephen Hendry, and chuffed that Ian Doyle had sent John Carroll to watch me.

I do exhibitions now and get people who want to slow down the game and play snookers, even though the crowd are there to see me get among the balls and make a hundred break. Sometimes you can't pot a ball for twenty minutes and it's embarrassing, and boring for the crowd.

Dad had dreamed of being a footballer when he was a kid, but by the time he met Mum he'd jacked it in and was trying to earn a few quid at Butlin's. The nearest he came to fulfilling his own sporting dream was when he played semi-pro football after he'd turned 30. A lot of his team-mates were much younger than him and used to call him Georgie Best the Second. I knew that nothing would have pleased him more than for me to become a professional sportsman. In a way, I thought, I would be living out his dream.

CHAPTER THREE

A Tragic Interlude

Chrissy Brooks was a great kid. He was 16, a couple of years older than me, and my doubles partner. We made a formidable team – virtually unbeatable. We won the Essex Pairs together year after year. I'd stay round his house at weekends, and we'd go to tournaments together. Chris's mum and dad, Mavis and Barry, used to drive him to the tournaments, and I caught a lift with them. After the tournament I used to go back to their house or down to the snooker club with them and have something to eat. Then they'd drop me off home on the Sunday night. I would be away all weekend with Chris, so we became very close.

We came through the junior ranks together and played together for six years. Doubles is a funny game. If you've got the wrong partner, if you're not relaxed with them, it can be nerve-racking. But Chris and I were a natural team. We trusted each other and we buzzed off each other. If one of us wasn't playing up to scratch the other one invariably was. And we both had a similar attitude to the game – we were attacking players, and if a shot was there to go for we went for it.

There was only really one tournament a year for us to enter, the Essex doubles. But we won it three years on the trot. We were unbeatable. I've often wondered what made us such a good team. In the end, I think it was because we were so close, we understood each other and trusted each other. Since Chris, I've never found a doubles partner like him. To be honest, I've not even found one I can play with. I've played with Jimmy, and even though we're great friends, somehow we can't do it as a team.

As we grew up I became increasingly passionate about snooker, about winning, and he went the opposite way. He had a girlfriend, wasn't practising as much as he used to and wasn't going to so many tournaments. We had a conversation one day that left its mark on me. He had just got himself a manager who was giving him money and paying all his entry fees, and he said to me, 'I just don't care if I win or lose. I only try if my manager's there watching me, but you just want to win because you want to win, because you love playing the game and you hate losing. I haven't got that.'

He was right. I was hungry to win, and it meant so much to me that he said that. He said he wished he had my attitude. He was always honest with himself and with others – he was one of the few kids playing snooker with me who never showed any jealousy. You can't be a champion without having that hunger, and I know I'm lucky to be the way I am. I never go into a match thinking I'm going to lose. I might think I'm not playing as well as I should be, but I still don't think I'll be beaten. It's only in the last few years that I've realised just how important this attitude is. If you have a good mental attitude, you don't need the greatest ability. I've seen players with all the talent in the world who don't have the attitude and they'll never make it. But people with the right attitude and decent ability can make it.

Look at someone like Dennis Taylor. He was World Champion but he's got no great natural ability. What he had was a hatred of losing. I remember playing him at Sheffield and he was an appalling loser. I thought, You're coming to the end of your career and I'm young, up and coming, and yet he had a proper sulk on. There are two chairs at Sheffield with an arm rest in between, and he sat straddling both chairs, not letting me sit down. We call him the Lobster because he always goes so red in the face when he's losing. I thought it was pathetic at the time, but without that attitude he would never have won a single tournament.

One day Chris and I were playing in a tournament in Birmingham, having driven up together as normal. He had already been beaten and I was 2-2 in my match. I said to Chris, 'Just wait for this frame and if I lose it I'm coming back with you.' I ended up winning it so never got in the car. Stuart Reardon, another snooker player from our club, was driving, and there was another fella in the car called Martin Caroline, who played at nearby Debden. They crashed. They'd come down from Birmingham with no problems and then realised that Martin had left his cue at his snooker club in Debden, so they rushed over there. The bend where they crashed is notorious. It's a 30 m.p.h. limit, but you can't take it at even that speed. Next day I was due to play in another tournament but my lift didn't show up. I phoned up one of the boys and asked, 'What's going on? You're meant to be here.'

'Haven't you heard?' he said. 'Chris and Martin have died in a car crash. Stuart was driving the car, but he survived.'

It didn't sink in. I went to the tournament and everybody was crying, but I didn't shed any tears. There was so much emotion around me but I just wanted to get on the snooker table. It didn't hit me until I went to the funeral with Mum, and I broke down. Mum, who believes in God, told me he'd be all right and that he was resting now, but I couldn't control my tears. Before the funeral I couldn't accept that it was happening, and then I saw people in their suits, paying their final respects, and I knew it was for real. It was the first time I realised I'd never see Chrissy again.

CHAPTER FOUR

Dad Goes to Prison

I left school without doing my exams. I'd always expected to turn professional, but it wasn't supposed to happen how it did. Even now I'd give anything to change the circumstances.

I suppose I was virtually a professional even when I was an amateur. After all, I'd been playing successfully in Pro-Am tournaments against professionals and travelling all over the country for a couple of years. I'd also picked up a manager. And not just any manager, but the legendary Barry Hearn, who managed my all-time hero, Steve Davis.

I first spoke to Barry just before I played in the English Amateur Championship final when I was 15. That was the tournament in which I made my first 147 – becoming the youngest person in history to make a maximum, by the way. In spite of the records I've broken since – like the fastest maximum of five minutes, twenty seconds – being the youngest player to make 147 is still my favourite. I reckon it'll stand for a while. Obviously it got a bit of publicity and my name must have become known because I was practising at home and Dad shouted from the house, 'There's someone on the phone for you.'

'Who is it?' I said.

'It's Barry Hearn,' came the reply.

I thought he was winding me up. Why would Barry Hearn call me?

'Hello, Ron,' he said. 'It's Barry here. Barry Hearn. And I've got two things to say to you. One, go and win the Amateur Championship on Saturday. And, two, I want to manage you.'

'Oh, all right then,' I said. I was gobsmacked. I didn't know what else to say. What do you do when you get a call from Barry Hearn? I also felt a bit sad. Until then, Dad had managed me, and it had always been me and him, but Dad was all for Barry taking over. If I was going to make it in the game, he knew that ultimately I'd need a proper manager, and Barry was the man.

'I've taken you as far as I can,' said Dad, 'and he's the biggest in the business. I just want the best for you.'

A couple of days later it was time for the English Amateurs final. I was up against a fella called Steve Judd, who was just a nutty potter – but he certainly outpotted me on that day. He won and I was gutted.

After the match Dad came up to me and said, 'Cheer up, Barry Hearn's here.'

Oh fuck, I thought, what am I going to say to him?

Barry came up to me and said, 'Never mind, chin up. Do you want to come up with me to Sheffield tomorrow?' While I'd been playing my final, the semi-finals of the World Championship had been going on at the Crucible.

'Yeah, dead right, I'd love to go up there.' It was the final in which John Parrott would go on to beat Jimmy White, who was managed by Barry, and it was when I would meet Jimmy's mates for the first time.

After Jimmy had beaten Steve James in the semis, Barry had come straight down to see me play in my final. I thought, Bloody hell, he must be serious. And he was. I signed a three-year contract with him, and then another one after that. A lot of people said Barry didn't care about the players, and he didn't come to any of the tournaments, but that suited me. I didn't want Barry sitting there in the front row while I was trying to win a title: that would have just been unnecessary pressure. I'd much rather be there on my own, with just my mate Del for company and support. Barry Hearn is the biggest charmer I've ever met in my life. He's genuine, straight to the point, calls a spade a spade, and won't waste his time.

But as far as I was concerned Dad was still there as my number one. The biggest change was that I started to be invited to more tournaments and exhibitions, which helped me to gain the experience I needed. Part of that experience involved travelling around the world, and a few months later I was playing in the World Amateur Championship in Thailand when I got a phone call from Mum. It came in the middle of the night, so I knew something serious had happened.

'I've got some news to tell you,' she said. 'I don't want you to do anything, everything's all right.'

'Well, what is it? Tell me, just tell me,' I said.

I knew it was something bad, but not in my wildest nightmares did I think it would be *this* bad.

'Daddy's been arrested,' she said. 'He's in police custody. He's been involved in a fight and someone's been killed.'

I just collapsed. I didn't know what to say, didn't know what to do. I started crying. Johnny O'Brien, who was still looking after me when I was on the road, took the phone out of my hand and spoke to Mum. Somehow, I knew that he already knew. I thought back to a week before we went to Thailand when we'd been in Amsterdam playing a competition, and there had been a phone call in the snooker club. Johnny went to answer it in the corner, and I could tell there was something wrong, but nothing was mentioned and I had forgotten about it until now.

I was winning everything at the time; things couldn't have been better. But almost as soon as I received that news I was gone. Weirdly, it didn't affect my game instantly. I went out to play and almost made a maximum – I'd potted thirteen reds and thirteen blacks, then missed a double on the next red, so I missed out on the £20,000 Volvo. For two or three games I was fine, then I started struggling. Mentally I was lost. I was in bits, didn't feel part of anything.

The previous week in Amsterdam I'd been flying. I was really excited on the night Johnny took the phone call in Amsterdam. I'd just won the tournament, just seen my old mate Chris Scanlon, and we'd gone out with Johnny to the red-light district. Next day we went home. We'd just moved house and Mum was running around like a nutcase, and I kept taking the piss out of her: 'Go on, businesswoman, you're flying here, you're flying there, you're flying everywhere,' I said.

'Shut up, Ronnie,' she said, 'I've got things to do.'

I was laughing because I didn't know what she was so flustered about.

Three days later she told me Barry wanted me to go out to Thailand a little bit earlier than planned.

'Why?' I said.

'Well, there's TV and a magazine wants to do an interview,' she replied: she knew exactly how to get me interested.

Brilliant, I thought. So I went out a week early, but when I arrived of course there was no TV, no magazine. I'd been there for two days and all we'd done was go down the snooker club and practise, which was great, but I was the only snooker player there and no one wanted me for an interview. I thought it was a bit strange, but I never in a million years thought that Mum had cooked up the story to get me out of the country. For three days after Mum's phone call I was all right on the surface, but then I crumbled. All I could think about was winning the tournament for Dad. It was just my way of coping with it. I suppose I thought that if I won the tournament, if I won everything, it would somehow make things better for him. I knew how much he loved me, how proud he was of me, and what a buzz he got from me doing well in snooker. I also knew he was well aware of how good I was, and what I could achieve, and that if I didn't achieve it I would have let him down and given him something else to feel guilty about. I couldn't let him down because he'd never let me down. My way of repaying him, and making him strong and happy, would be to succeed at snooker.

If that sounds like I kept myself together, I didn't. Mentally, I was lost. I can see it now, but I couldn't back then. I was playing the Welshman David Bell, and my concentration was so bad I had to stick a penny on the floor to try to get my head together. I'd never done it before, but I thought it was better than staring at the floor, which is what I had been doing. I was in a daze. My mind was blank. I stared and stared at this penny, but it didn't do any good. David beat me 4–3, and I cried when I lost. I'd never done that before, either.

It dawned on me then that Mum and Barry had sent me to Thailand early because they thought that by the time I got back Dad would be home, everything would be sorted, and it would all have been a horrible mistake that I didn't need to know about. Then Barry had said to Mum, 'This is for real. I think you'd better phone Ronnie and tell him what's happening.'

The whole time we'd been in Thailand I'd felt that something wasn't right between me and Johnny. He never put his arm round me, didn't treat me as he usually did. I discovered later that his brother was also nicked with Dad, but in the end he was done just for affray. Perhaps Johnny didn't know what pain I was in out there, but he never offered any support. I ended up not talking to him, not even being able to look at him.

After I'd been knocked out I smashed my cue against the hotel corridor wall and I started crying again. I phoned Mum. 'I've let him down, I've let him down,' I said.

'You've not let anyone down,' she said. 'We love you, and Daddy's going to be all right. Make sure you're all right. Get on the plane, come home, and we'll go and visit Daddy.'

That was all I wanted to do: see Daddy.

'Sort out what you've got to sort out,' said Mum, 'and we'll pick you up from the airport, and we'll go together.'

Barry Hearn's driver, Robbo, drove Mum to the airport, and they picked us up. We then went straight to the nick: we pulled up outside Brixton Prison in a stretch limo! I'd never been in a prison in my life, and it was a shock. I couldn't believe Dad was stuck in there. As soon as I saw him, I thought, This isn't my dad. He was wearing a prisoner's uniform and was looking rough because he'd been in a cell for two weeks, all told. He hadn't been eating properly and he looked pale. He'd always been so happy and positive, but here he looked like any other prisoner, just a number.

I grabbed him and said, 'We're going to get you

out of here, we're going to get you out of here.' I was crying, and he had a little tear coming down his face, too. I'd never seen him cry before.

'All that's nothing,' he said. 'I'm here now. You just concentrate and be good for Mum. Mum's all right, and I'm all right and don't you worry about me. You visit me and write to me, and I'll write to you.'

It was cutting me up. Thinking about it even now I well up. It seems like yesterday.

We got to see him for only twenty minutes. 'Give us a kiss, give us a hug,' said Dad. I was crying and he was waving, and I couldn't bear it.

After that visit we drove straight to my school. I saw Mrs Abbot, the deputy head, and she already knew what had happened – presumably Mum had told her.

Mum said to her: 'He's going to be having a bit of time off. Ronnie's not going to be coming to school.'

'Fine,' she said. 'We know what you're going through. You just take a bit of time and sort yourself out.'

And that was it. I never went back to school. It was halfway through the first term of the fifth year, my GCSE year. Almost as soon as I left I got my first proper girlfriend, Pippa, the girl Robert Chapman had tried to set me up with in Hastings years before and who I'd been too nervous even to look at. We met up at the snooker club on a Thursday night soon after Dad was charged, and it was the first time I'd seen her since those lustful longings when I was 10.

I took her back home and said, 'I'm going to Belgium on Saturday, d'you want to come?' I hadn't even kissed her. She said yes, and I thought, This could be it. We flew to Belgium and after we landed, in the car to the hotel, I put my arms round her and kissed her. From the minute we arrived at the hotel I only got out of bed for the snooker. It was the best weekend I'd ever had, and I won the tournament and a grand, too!

Each evening at about 6 p.m. I could barely stay awake because I'd hardly had any sleep, but by 11 p.m. I just came to life. I was like a bat. I played some of the best snooker I'd ever played. In one match I was up against the Belgian champion, Steve Lemings. His manager owned the club, the game was on TV and there were about six hundred people in the venue, almost all of them wanting me to get beat. Pippa was there in the back row, though, and it gave me a real buzz knowing she was watching me. I loved it: the underdog, the outsider, and with my girlfriend looking on. Perfect. I won 4–3.

Aside from Pippa, perhaps the only person who wanted me to win was my big Belgian fan, a young, little woman, almost a dwarf, who'd come with a couple of her friends. Later, after I'd turned professional, every time I played in Belgium she would be sitting there in the front row, and she always gave me little gifts. I'll never forget her because she was so devoted – if I was getting beat you could see the sadness in her face.

Although I won in Belgium, as soon as things

started getting serious with Pippa I started losing. I wasn't even winning matches in Pro-Ams. I'd been messing around for about five months, concentrating on her rather than snooker, when Dad came out on bail in February 1992. I was at the snooker club when I got the call from Mum. She was ringing around asking all the people she knew with money if they could put up a surety for Dad. It was a Friday afternoon and if we didn't get down to the prison in time he would have had to stay in there for the weekend. So everyone was rushing around getting their money together. His bail was half a million pounds.

The family of my old snooker mate Robert Chapman were brilliant when Dad went down. My parents and his used to speak to each other on the phone all the time, because Robert was either at my house or I was at his, but amazingly they had never met, even though we'd been mates for years. The first time Mum met his parents was after Dad had been charged. Ray, Robert's dad, put up bail for Dad, and Angie, his mum, looked after my sister when Mum was away in prison later. But that's another story.

Michael Leech, one of my mates from Leeds who had come down to visit, drove me to the prison. There were about thirty people standing outside Brixton Prison gates. The gates opened and Dad was just standing there: he was so skinny. He was carrying a big wooden box with all our letters to him, and all the bits and pieces he'd kept. Everyone cheered. We rushed over, and he gave Mum a big hug, and I just stood there and watched. Then he gave me a big hug, and I squeezed him.

In the car on the way home it was the first time I'd seen Mum and Dad together in about six months, and I thought, Things are going to be OK. We're a family again.

Our house was packed with about forty people, and we were up until around 1 a.m. I was exhausted and told Dad that I had to go to bed because I had a competition in the morning in Wickford – a little Pro-Am, thirty entries, four hundred quid to the winner. At eight o'clock in the morning he walked into my bedroom, immaculate. He'd had a shower, he was back in his old gear, and I was looking at him thinking, Fucking hell, Dad, you never normally get out of bed till noon. He'd told me the night before he would wake me up in the morning. 'Are you sure?' I'd asked. 'Because you're not normally too clever at getting up.' But after six months of prison, he had no trouble getting out of bed in the morning. 'Come on,' he said, 'we're going to Wickford.'

We drove to Wickford in his blue Mercedes. There was some music playing – 'Real Gone Kid' by Deacon Blue. When it was playing I noticed he had another tear rolling down his cheek. He didn't want me to see it, so he brushed it away carefully, but it set me off anyway.

When we walked in at Wickford, everyone was amazed to see him. They all knew him, and most of them were more friendly with him than they were with me because he was such a character. They were delighted to see him.

I was knackered, but I was playing on pure adrenalin. During the semi-finals Dad said he would have to miss the final because he had to go and sign on at the police station at home. I felt terrible because I knew he would be gutted to leave. I beat Mark King in the final 4–1 with a couple of centuries and an 80. I was playing great snooker for the first time in months. Suddenly it all clicked.

During his time out on bail, Dad sat me down and said, 'Right, you don't want to go back to school, do you?'

'No,' I said.

'Well, if you're leaving school, you've got to do what I say. That means you're up at nine in the morning, you've got to do a three-mile run every day, go down the snooker club, do your practice, home for your dinner, in bed by ten. That's the deal or you're going back to school.'

'I'll take the snooker,' I said.

But I was still messing around, and still seeing Pippa.

'Look,' he said, 'you either want to succeed or you don't want to succeed. You've got to make your mind up between Pippa and the snooker.'

I exploded. 'I'm in love with her,' I said. 'Fuck the snooker. I'll do what I want to do when I want to do it.'

'OK,' he said, 'I'll ring Barry Hearn now and tell him you're not interested in playing snooker. I'm going to tell him you're not turning professional in June.'

'Yeah, go on, do that,' I said, 'and I'll just ring Ian Doyle. He'll manage me. Anyone will manage me.'

Mum was sitting there with Dad, and we argued it out for two hours. I thought, Whatever they say to me, they're never going to tell me what to do again. I rebelled and rebelled. Dad hated the fact that I was messing about. He thought I was on the verge of throwing away everything I had in front of me. Eventually, I stormed out of the room.

Quite a while later Dad came up to me and gave me a big hug. 'I fucking love you,' he said.

'I love you, too,' I said.

'Right, we're going to crack this together. We're a team, aren't we?'

That was it. We'd cleared the air and sorted it out. I would still go out with Pippa, but I was going to be a professional snooker player. If she didn't like it, that was tough. But she said she didn't mind at all. I was the one making an issue of it. I'd decided I was doing it my way. I probably felt ashamed to tell Pippa that I was still doing what my dad told me to do. After all, I was 16 now and thought I had to be a man, stand up for myself and tell my dad I'd see whoever I wanted to see.

I started practising again and my game came back together. In June I went to play my qualifiers at Norbreck Castle in Blackpool for the World Championship. Johnny O'Brien was still my chaperone, and we'd also made up. Dad had been out on bail for a few months and whipped me into shape. I was still going out with Pippa, but I knew I was going to be away for at least three months. If I lost a few matches I'd get a chance to go home maybe three or four times during the whole three and a half months in Blackpool. As it turned out, I got a chance to go home early once, which was after the first week. I'd played six matches and qualified, and I went home. But Pippa wasn't happy with me being away, and when I'd gone back up to Blackpool I got a phone call from her saying we were finished.

'Look, I'm coming home straight away and we'll talk about it,' I said.

'No, don't bother,' she said and put the phone down.

I went to bed, devastated.

By now, a quarter of the way through the qualifiers, Dad's bail restrictions were eased. He had to sign on twice a day, and he asked the police if he could do it in Blackpool for a couple of weeks. He got the go-ahead, so he came up to see me, with Mum and my little sister, Danielle. Next day I was playing a match and I went 3–0 down. I nicked one back to go in 3–1 down at the break. As I came out, Dad said, 'Are you all right?'

'No, I'm not,' I replied. 'Something's happened.'

'What's the matter?'

'Me and Pippa. We're finished.'

'What, it's all over?' I nodded. 'Don't worry about that. This is what's important. Forget about her.

You're going to have untold women on your case. Just go out there and play your snooker, and over the next couple of years you're going to have them flocking. First love!'

'Yeah, you're right,' I said, even though I didn't think he was. I went out and won the match 5–3. And from that moment onwards, I didn't even think about it.

If Dad hadn't been there, I would have definitely lost that match and I'd have gone back to London and tried to save the relationship. I found out later that she had met someone else, but I suppose that was to be expected – I'd already been away for six weeks and there was a good chance I'd be up there for another six.

I did an article for the *Sun* while I was in Blackpool. I told the interviewer that I'd had trials for Tottenham but wasn't really interested because I was so dedicated to snooker. It wasn't quite true – I was never good enough to make it as a footballer. I then went on to say that I had chucked my girlfriend because it was getting in the way of my snooker. And there it was in black and white in the *Sun*. About a year later Pippa phoned me and said, 'What was all that about in the *Sun*? You chucked me?'

'Yeah,' I said, 'I thought I'd get you back.'

'I was sitting on the beach with all my mates in Tenerife, and I read this article that said you'd done this and done that, and I thought, You lying bastard,' she said.

'Well, I got you back, didn't I?' I said.

We had a laugh about it and I saw her a few times after that, but by then I was over her.

I believe that certain things happen for a reason, and you're destined to do what you're supposed to do. I'd only recovered my form because Dad had got bail and knocked me into shape. I think if he'd not got bail and not been there for me, I would have gone downhill very quickly. I wouldn't have won as many matches as I did that year, I'd have qualified for only one or two tournaments, and I would have returned to snooker the year after in an even more despairing state of mind. As a player, I would have been starting from scratch; and maybe I'd still be trying to make the relationship with Pippa work. Since then I've occasionally had relationships that I've tried to hang on to and it's always affected my game.

I had so much success in that first professional season, 1992–3, that I went from number 800 in the world to 57. I won 74 out of 76 matches, which was a record. That's all I was going for then – records. Every time I went out I was thinking, What's the next record? I beat Stephen Hendry's record of consecutive victories. OK, it wasn't against the top pros, but to win thirty-eight matches on the trot is going some by any standard. I also broke the record for the quickest match, which I won 5–0 in 43 minutes in Blackpool. I was 4–0 up after half an hour, and I came out and nobody could believe that I was on the interval. Back on the table I made a 70 break in no time, but the fella didn't concede. The longer the game went on the less chance I had of breaking Tony Drago's record, but there was nothing I could do about it: he just kept playing. I had the hump. I was 80 points up with 59 left on, so he needed five or six snookers, and I felt like saying to him, 'Put your cue away, you can't win, you're ruining any chance of a record here.' In the end I beat Drago's record by five minutes.

I could certainly be nippy around a table and around this time Alan Hughes, the snooker MC, said, 'Ronnie, I've got to give you a nickname.'

'Nah, Ronnie's just fine,' I said.

'No, you've got the Whirlwind and you've got the Hurricane. I want to call you the Rocket!'

'You're having a laugh, aren't you?' I said. 'You can't call me the Rocket. It's corny.'

'No,' he said, 'it's perfect for you. And when you're playing really well I'm going to call you Red Hot Rocket!'

The nickname stuck, of course. I suppose it was appropriate when I made the fastest maximum in history in the World Championship in 1997 – five minutes, twenty seconds. Even I've got no idea how I did it that fast, though, and I've never come close to that time since. It was just silly speed and I can't see it ever being beaten. Red Hot was right!

Dad was where he was meant to be when he came to see me in Blackpool as I tried to qualify for my first World Championship. Although it was a terrible thing that happened to him, and a terrible thing that he did, I try to look at it positively now. It's made me who I am, and made him who he is, and hopefully when he comes out he'll have learned who his true friends are and who is worth trusting. I think one of his problems was that he was too generous, too trusting.

When he was out on bail and all those people were there to celebrate his homecoming, one of them asked to borrow quite a bit of money. Once Dad was sentenced we never saw that fella again. He still owes Dad the money. I hope when Dad comes out he'll remember which people took him for a ride, and which people said Mum wouldn't be able to deal with the business on her own. There were too many people who wanted to be with Dad because he was a spend-freak. Mum's filtered out the false friends over the years since Dad has been away, and now she counts only Angie and Ray Chapman as true friends, the type you can rely on when the chips are really down.

While I was still in Blackpool, Dad had to return down south because the trial was about to start. I had three days between matches and rushed back to London to see him. I got home about 1 a.m. and must have got him out of bed. He came downstairs and he looked awful. I'd never seen Dad with cold sores before, but he had a massive one on his face. It must have been stress, but he hardly ever let on about the pressure he was under. The few times he did mention it, he simply said, 'I'm coming home.

I'm not guilty, I'm coming home.' But perhaps the cold sore told another story.

Mum didn't talk much about the trial either. Like many families, we never used to speak about anything much in the house. We often covered up about things we should have discussed. There was always the sense that you can't show you're weak, that an admission of weakness is a weakness in itself. Our philosophy was 'We must be positive, we must move forward.' I now think that's wrong. Yes, you have to move on, and you can't turn back the clock, but there were things we should have discussed that we just bottled up. We were never prepared for Dad going away. He never sat me down and said, 'Look, I could be going away for twenty years. How are you going to deal with it?' He was so confident that he wasn't going to be convicted that he even bought another shop during the trial. Recently, he said to me, 'That was a good move!'

'What d'you mean, that was a good move?' I asked. 'A good move would have been you coming home.'

'No,' he said. 'Getting that shop sorted was a good move. Halfway through the trial someone came in, gave me the nod, and I bought the shop in Brewer Street, and that was a right good one. That's what's kept Mum going while I've been away. That was the bread and butter.'

He never thought about himself: he just wanted to make sure that everything was all right financially. But we never sorted out anything emotionally. We never prepared for what might happen; we always dealt with issues as they happened or later. It's still like that today to a great extent.

On 20 September 1992 I beat Mark Jonson-Allen to qualify for the next year's World Championship after three and a half months at Blackpool. The next day I went back to London. Dad was in prison as the case had already started at the Old Bailey. In fact, it was coming to an end: the defence and prosecution had summed up, and after three weeks of listening to the case the jury had retired.

I was sitting in my granddad's house with him and his mate Alfie waiting for the verdict. When my auntie Barbara walked in I knew by the look on her face that it wasn't good news. The jury had found Dad guilty of murder and the judge sentenced him to life. The judge recommended that he should serve eighteen years, which is six years more than the average recommendation. In his summing up the judge referred to 'racial overtones', which I think is why he added on the extra six years. Now, how the judge decided that Dad was a racist I will never understand. He got it so wrong. Dad grew up in Hackney among black kids and he's probably got more black friends than he has white friends. Going down as a racist was, for him, almost as bad as going down as a murderer. Not only was it untrue, he got a hell of a lot of stick for it at first in prison before the other inmates found out the truth. The judge's comments and the verdict demonised him: being labelled a racist is up there with being a rapist and a paedophile in the nick.

It was a long time before I learned what had happened in the incident: how there had been a fight in a nightclub and an argument over the bill. Dad and his mate were arguing over which of them would pay their bill. Then two black fellas, brothers who had been signed in that night by Charlie Kray, got the wrong end of the stick and thought Dad and his mate weren't going to pay. A row started. Dad said, 'Let's talk about it,' and walked round the bar, where one of the brothers picked up an ashtray and went to whack Dad over the head. Dad put up his hand, the ashtray smashed, and two of his fingers were severed. The other fella then picked up a champagne bottle and smashed Dad over the head with it. Dad then picked up a knife that was on the side of the bar and that was it.

Dad was in hospital for four days. The police wanted him discharged earlier but the sister on the ward flatly refused. When the police finally arrested Dad, he never admitted that he had stabbed the guy. That was stupid. He should have simply said yes, he had done it, and it was an act of self-defence. But he was terrified of going down.

The idea that it was murder, let alone a racist murder, didn't bear thinking about. The prosecution never claimed the attack was racially motivated, but somehow the judge in his infinite wisdom seemed to have presumed that if a black man was killed by a white man, he must have been killed because of the colour of his skin. Quite a few prominent black people, like Nigel Benn, as well as black mates of

Dad's, offered to testify in court that Dad was no racist. One of them, Vince, is a black barber and Dad is godfather to his daughter. (These days Dad sends all his black mates from prison to Vince's for a good haircut when they get out.) They all said they wanted to bear witness to his character, but Dad was too proud to accept their help. A lot of his black mates come up to me now and say, 'It's bollocks. Your dad is no racist. He knows the score. He's not got a racist bone in his body.' The Prison Service tried to make it extra hard for him by sending him to a prison full of black inmates. It was difficult for him initially, but it soon got round among the black men in the system that Ronnie O'Sullivan Senior is a good man. They even put him on the Jamaican food boat for chicken, rice and peas. They love him in there.

But black people come up to me even now and accuse Dad of being a racist, and they've wanted to start on me. How can I explain to someone who's angry, and who knows what the judge said, that Dad isn't what he was made out to be?

Perhaps Dad's downfall was that he never said a word throughout the trial. Every time he was asked something by the police, he answered, 'No comment, no comment, no comment.' So he never told his story. It was no surprise to me because when I was a kid he told me that if I was ever questioned by the police I should keep my mouth shut. (One day the police came to visit the school. An officer asked me my name, and I said, 'No comment.' I couldn't understand why everyone laughed.) He was convinced he was right, that he knew best, but he didn't. In court it made him look as if he had something to hide. It's all very well talking about the right to silence, as he did in those days, but it's not as simple as that.

Yes, he had a right to silence, but the judge and jury also had the right to interpret it as an admission of guilt, as they so often do. It was the worst thing he could have done. It was common sense to get up in the dock and say, 'Look, I was attacked, he hit me first and I had to fight back. Unfortunately, I went too far and killed the man.' But he never said a word, and it proved disastrous.

He knows his mistake now. But you can't turn back the clock. Sometimes I replay the court case in my head and this time he tells the jury and the judge everything; he proves he's not a racist; and illustrates how what he did was an act of self-defence.

After the trial Dad's barrister's assistant said to me, 'Your dad is one of the strongest people I've ever come across in my job.' She told me Dad had said to her, ' "I just want you to tell my boy two things: that I love him and that he should just go and win." ' He never shed a tear. 'I can't believe how strong a man he is. I've been in this job for many years, and I've never seen the courage of someone like that before,' she told me.

Mum said when he was found guilty he blew her a kiss, said, 'I love you,' and didn't show one bit of emotion. When I heard that it made me go weak.

I still carry all those things people say about him

today. I know he is a strong man, and in a way I wish he wasn't because it would make life much easier for me. The way he's done his time makes me feel inadequate – it makes me think I've got to get my act together. How can he cope as well as he does when I can't even cope with life on the outside?

Dad has already had one appeal against his sentence rejected, but we are still fighting on to prove that even if we accepted it was murder, which we don't, he shouldn't be serving any more than the normal tariff – especially because he's been a model prisoner. We are saying that eighteen years for killing a man in a fight goes far beyond what a man would usually have to serve. Sometimes I think he received such a harsh sentence because he was my dad, and I was well known, and also because his business was sex shops.

CHAPTER FIVE

Losing Mum

It was 1993, Dad was banged up and life was complicated at best, a mess at worst. Despite all the terrible things that had happened in 1992, in many ways it was my golden year: all those records beaten, the 38-match unbeaten run, the 22 times I'd whitewashed opponents 5–0, Dad out on bail to watch me at Blackpool turning over player after player. But now he was in jail doing his time and I felt a huge sense of loss. Dad had always been such a huge part of my everyday life. He supported me, made me laugh, bollocked me when I did wrong and he still did his best when he was inside, but it wasn't the same. I felt fragile and vulnerable, ill at ease with myself.

I was determined to treat my body with respect, look after it as a professional sportsman should. I was down the gym or running every day, trying to eat healthily and not drink and smoke. But it wasn't easy. I knew that with a bit of a drink in me I became more relaxed in company.

I was only 17, but I worried that my snooker had already peaked and I was on a downward spiral. Somehow, in 1992, every shot I took, every choice I made, I just knew instinctively was right. But now everything seemed much more of a struggle.

Yet to the outside world it looked just the opposite. In 1992, no one outside the snooker halls knew my name, but by the end of 1993 I was becoming famous, touted as the new people's champion, the heir to Alex 'Hurricane' Higgins and Jimmy 'Whirlwind' White. I was already a name. And even though I knew I wasn't playing anywhere near as well as I could do, I was playing good enough snooker to rocket up the rankings. As far as the outside world was concerned, there was only one way I could go: forward.

In November 1993, I reached the final of the UK Championship at the Guild Hall in Preston. I was 17 years and 11 months old, and playing Stephen Hendry, the undisputed world number one, in the final. It was one of those matches when everything clicked. I was back playing on instinct again, just like at Blackpool. Stephen made 44 in the first frame then had a bit of bad luck with a couple of shots, and I cleared up with a 78. He was also first to score in the second frame, but after his opening 23 I knocked in 103, Stephen responded with a 132 and then scored 73 to draw equal at 2–2, then I took all four in the afternoon, including a break of 121. Three centuries in a major final – this was as good as it got. In the evening I played solidly and scored consistently: 62, 73 and finally an 85. I had beaten Stephen 10–6 and won seventy grand. A week short of my 18th birthday and I had seventy grand! I couldn't believe it. I wondered if I'd get a call from my old head teacher asking me to take the cheque into school to show his mate.

I was buzzing, and I just thought, I want more of this: that brilliant feeling of a packed house, sweating with tension, and nearly everyone rooting for me. I'd beaten Steve Davis and Stephen Hendry in one tournament, the two greatest players in snooker history, and I was in a state of blissful shock. I'd even trimmed nine months off Stephen Hendry's record to become the youngest ever winner of a ranking tournament.

Suddenly I was back-page news in the newspapers. Every profile seemed to start with my vital statistics: first century at 10, first 147 at 15, 38 matches unbeaten, etc. It was only when I read it like that I began to have any sense of what I'd achieved.

The snooker commentator Clive Everton wrote an article in which he talked about my 'confidence, fluency and fearlessness', and said that I was a model of dedication to my sport. I was well chuffed, although I wasn't sure how true it was. In one way, it was. I did practise and practise all day long from mid-morning till late into the evening, and I was still relatively fearless on the table. I'd risen from 57th in the rankings into the top 16, which meant that I automatically qualified for all the major tournaments.

Straight after the final, Clive asked me what I was going to do now that I'd won the UK. I grinned, and told him that tomorrow I was going to visit Dad with the trophy, and enjoy the best two hours of my life with him. Next day Dad and I had a great time. He was proud of me, and wasn't afraid to say so.

In Clive's article he also described me as 'friendly, cheerful and astonishingly self-possessed', which made me laugh. Again, it was true in a way: when I felt good I was friendly and cheerful. But already there were times, away from the table, when I was in pieces. For starters, I wanted Dad back. And second, although I'd dreamed of a time when strangers would come up to me in clubs, recognise me, and start chatting away, when it actually happened it wasn't that easy. I felt as shy and awkward as ever, unless I had a drink in me.

Five months later, in April 1994, I won the British Open at the Plymouth Pavilions. I beat James Wattana 9–4 in the final, and it was my second major title of the season. Only Stephen Hendry and Steve Davis had won more than one title that season, and now I was being talked about in the same breath. World rankings are based on the previous season's results coupled with the current season, which meant that if I showed a bit of form I'd be number three in the world by next year. With the thirty-six grand from the British, I'd taken my winnings for the season to £165,000. I'd been making a decent living from snooker for five years by now, but this was a different league. I treated myself to a top-of-the-range BMW. This was the first time I'd really enjoyed my winnings. As a kid, I never saw much of the cash I won, and, to be honest, it was never a priority for me. I was in it for the trophies, the glory.

People had started taking bets on when I was going to win my first world championship. Barry Hearn was going around telling everyone that it wasn't a matter of if but when. He reckoned it was going to be this year. To be fair, even Ian Doyle, who had failed to sign me, was saying pretty much the same, except that he reckoned it would take me a couple of years longer.

Whenever I was interviewed I was asked about Dad. I told reporters how close we were, how he had been my inspiration and that he wasn't a bad man despite what had happened. Dad had always told me to talk the talk and walk the walk, and whenever I was interviewed I tried my best. I told journalists that I wasn't going to feel sorry for myself just because Dad was away, that I was old enough and ugly enough to look after myself, which were Dad's words exactly. At times, I thought I was beginning to sound like him. I told the press that Dad was in prison and he had a sentence to do and he was gonna do it like a man rather than cry like a baby, and that my head wasn't going to drop because he was in there. Dad had told me that if I wanted to make him proud I had to keep my chin up, and go out and do the best that I could, be an ambassador for the sport. And that's what I told people I was doing when they asked.

Journalists seemed surprised that I was so upfront about Dad. I don't know if they expected me to deny that he was inside or to cut myself off from him. They were amazed when I told them that he was going to run my fan club, and that the address to write to was: Ronnie O'Sullivan Snr, D-wing, Wormwood Scrubs. I didn't see what was so weird about it. At least fans weren't likely to forget the address.

I did sound so confident when I talked to journalists. But most of it was front. Inside I was doing the opposite. I was crying like a baby, and I was beginning to crack up.

Of course, I didn't win the World Championship that year. Nor for many years afterwards. I got to the last sixteen and was slaughtered 13–3 by John Parrott. But I did win the WBSA Young Player of the Year Award for 1993 and went on to be voted Player of the Year for 1994. On paper, things couldn't have been better. All the experts were predicting that I'd start to dominate the game. But it didn't happen. There were too many off days both on and off the table.

I was 18 years old, almost 19, and the game was getting me down. Towards the end of the year, I announced that I was seriously considering quitting snooker because it was making me unhappy. It didn't seem anything like the game I'd played for love as a kid, and I was nowhere near hitting the heights of that first year at Blackpool. I no longer felt, when I went out, that I was going to automatically win the match; and if I didn't feel I was the best, what was the point of playing?

All the players and experts said I wasn't serious, and that I'd be around for years. But I was very serious. Every time I've considered giving the game up I've been serious about it. Ultimately, though, they were proved right: I didn't quit and I have been around for years.

Just after Dad was convicted, it appeared that the police were doing a Big Brother job on us when they started investigating Mum. They watched us for the next eighteen months and by 1994 obviously had everything they needed.

Bizarrely, things again reached crisis point when I was playing in a tournament in Thailand. My mate picked me up from the airport when I got home. 'You're never going to guess what's happened now,' he said.

'What's that?'

'Your mum's in the nick for tax evasion.'

'You're having a laugh, aren't you? You are joking me,' I said.

'I'm not,' he said. 'Little Danielle's with us at the moment, and your mum's in Lime Street Police Station.' He told me that the police had stormed the house at 5 a.m. and carted her off to the station.

They wouldn't let me visit Mum for four days. All I could do was speak to her lawyer and send her down some clothes and food. After four days she was up in front of a judge at the Old Bailey applying for bail. That's when I phoned Barry Hearn. 'They want a million bail,' I said. 'You've got to help me out here.'

'Right! You go off to court,' he said. 'Let me know if you need me, and if you do I'll be straight down there.'

'I know we need you,' I said.

Within forty-five minutes he was there, and he gave one of the most brilliant speeches I've ever heard. The judge asked him if he could afford the bail. 'Well,' he said, 'I'm the manager of twelve snooker players, I am the owner of a three-million-pound house, I am the owner of a business that turns over twenty million pounds a year, so I think that qualifies me for putting up a million pounds in bail.' Everyone in the court cracked up.

I love Barry and I was so glad he was still my manager at that point and could do that for Mum and me. I say that because I'd almost deserted him the year before.

My contract was coming up for renewal, and John Carroll, Ian Doyle's right-hand man, started getting all pally with me again. Eventually they offered me £100,000 a year just to sign up with them. This was just a couple of years after I'd turned pro, of course, and at the time I was getting considerably less from Barry. John Carroll had come down from Scotland and taken me and Mum out to a restaurant, and it sounded pretty tempting.

I spoke to Dad just before I went to see Barry about the new contract. He said, 'Look, whatever you do, do not sign a contract. What you do with

Barry is shake his hand, and say, "You've got me for another year." Don't sign any contract at all.' He said that I should do the year and then I'd be free to talk to whoever I fancied.

I went into the office to talk to Barry, 18 and naïve as you like.

Barry sat me down and said, 'Right, are you going to sign another contract, then?'

Before I could stop myself, I said, 'Yeah, yeah, yeah, I'll sign another contract.'

He put the contract in front of me, and despite everything Dad had said I felt obliged to sign it. I thought if I didn't sign it he'd think I didn't like him or something.

When I got home Dad phoned up and said, 'Well, how did you get on?'

'I signed,' I mumbled.

'You fucking arsehole.'

'Well, Dad, he put it in front of me and . . .' I didn't know what to say because I didn't know why I'd signed it myself.

'Look, don't worry about it. Just get on with your snooker.'

It was a right balls-up. I was meant to sign with Ian Doyle. I never promised him, but I had said to John Carroll that it sounded good, although I needed time to think about it. In the contract meeting with Barry I told him that Ian Doyle had sent John down to try to poach me. Barry had obviously got straight on the phone to Ian and slagged him off because Ian called me and said, 'Don't you ever tell anybody about John Carroll coming down to see you. You've caused a right load of trouble.'

I didn't know what I'd done wrong, so I had a bit of a barney with Ian, and that was it. For the next three years I stayed with Barry Hearn.

It was crazy really. I could have used Ian Doyle's approach to force Barry to give me a better offer, but I just signed the usual contract with no guarantees. Then he told me I was going to be his pension in years to come. Later, Ian Doyle tried to use that against him. He told me, 'I'd never say that about one of my players. I think it was totally out of order that Barry said such a thing.' But I didn't know what he was making such a fuss about. I just thought, Well, I hope I am his pension, because if I am it means I ain't doing too bad.

He's done things for me that I don't think Ian Doyle, who managed me later in my career, would have been able to do for me. Right from the very start Barry Hearn was in it with me through thick and thin, helping me and my family both on and off the table. He was always at the end of the phone when a crisis came up. He was a great manager for me. All right, he never produced great sponsorship deals off the table, but I have massive respect for him because he was always there when I needed him, sorting out problems as and when they came up.

When the police raided Mum's house they got hold of all the books and paperwork and took them away. After Dad had gone inside, Mum wasn't really the best person to be dealing with the money side of things – she didn't understand it because she had never had to. Her main concerns were keeping the family together and keeping the roof over our heads. When the authorities told her she owed a fortune in VAT and other taxes she was genuinely shocked. She paid it all off but they still sent her to prison for evasion. Watching her being sentenced on the day she was finally sent down in late '95 was one of the worst experiences of my life. I couldn't work out why she had to go down now that she'd coughed up what they reckoned was owing. I think it was a conspiracy against the family.

She was sentenced to a year in prison and served seven months. The morning before she was convicted I had to go off to talk to someone about the sex shops and sort out various bits and pieces. I went down to the court in the afternoon with my mate Steve. He had first-hand experience of the courts and knew how they worked. I asked him what was going on and he drew in his breath and said it didn't look good.

'What d'you mean?' I said.

'She's going down.'

'What? She's going in the nick?'

Mum was standing in the dock. She couldn't hear what we were whispering.

When the jury returned its verdict and the judge said, 'Take her down,' she looked at me and I burst into tears. She didn't cry, though. I expected her to, but she didn't.

Weirdly, it was a good thing that she went away,

because after prison she understood everything Dad was talking to her about: the day-to-day routine of his life. He'd be on the phone, and say to her, 'Maria, I've got to go, they're kicking off in there, you know.' And she knew exactly what he meant because she'd been through it herself.

When they were both inside, Mum and Dad ended up in the same court, both of them charged with selling obscene magazines and videos. In the break for lunch the two of them were put into a cell together and had an hour to themselves. For the next six weeks of the trial, they were sitting together. Dad just laughed his way through the whole thing. He was made up to be with Mum again, however temporary it was. He kept nudging the prosecution barristers and having a giggle with them.

Halfway through the trial, one of the tabloids printed a story saying that Mum was already in prison serving a sentence for tax evasion. It was obvious contempt of court and prejudiced the case against her, so they had to release her. The judge said, 'Mrs O'Sullivan, you are free to go,' but she didn't want to leave Dad.

Dad said, 'Go on, you're off now, get going,' and she did, but she told me later, 'I was so happy with your dad there, I didn't want to go.'

My world was turned upside down with Mum inside. I'd never looked after anyone before, not even myself. All I'd had to do while she was around was come in, eat my dinner, put on my freshly washed and ironed clothes, and play snooker. Then suddenly

In the house in Ilford, where Dad built me my own snooker room.

Dad consoling me after I lost the English Amateur Final. Had I won it, I would have been the youngest ever winner. That honour rests with my good mate Jimmy White.

The World Junior Under-21s in India. The one moment in the tournament when I felt I just might, against the odds, get beaten.

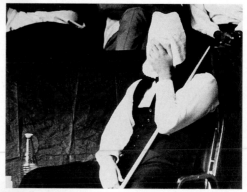

Back at home at my snooker HQ (i.e., Mum and Dad's house) with both the highest break trophy and the World Junior trophy.

I had to take care not only of myself but of my sister Danielle. I was 19, and Danielle was 12, and I was trying to keep hold of things, making out that everything was OK, but it wasn't. Danielle would go to school and I'd try to cook her a meal when she came home, but I'd never done any cooking outside of school home economics classes before. So we got by on oven chips, fish fingers and beans. I didn't have a driving licence at the time because I'd lost it through speeding, so I couldn't even take her to and from school. We were in a mess . . . and I panicked.

It was difficult to get out with Danielle at home, so I reckoned the best solution was to invite people over and throw some parties. For the last couple of years, as I'd got more successful, and won myself a few quid, we'd gone to hotels and it had cost a fortune. So I thought, We'll save a few quid here, just get a load of vodka in, a load of dope, and use this as a party gaff. Mum had been away only a week when I had the first party. I invited everybody – even people I didn't know. I just thought, Now that I've got this big house to myself I must have a party, pretend it's mine, and impress everyone. I had the barbecue going even though it was pissing down with rain, and we were all off our faces. When I look back on it now it terrifies me because I was really losing the plot. At the end of the evening people said, 'Well, we better be getting off,' and I told them they couldn't leave yet. Eventually, after partying for two days, they went home.

After a good sleep I woke up and looked at the

house. There were thousands of empty bottles of Bud everywhere and burn holes from where people had stubbed out their fags. The place looked like a bomb had hit it. Mum is a cleanliness freak and she keeps the gaff spotless. If she'd seen the place she'd have killed me. I started picking up all the bottles, but didn't really know where to start. So I got on the phone to my mate Fred, and asked him to come round. I knew he was handy with a duster, good around a bit of cleaning. He used to help Mum out, when he lived with us for a while, some time ago. He drove a tank in the army, then worked with kids in a nursery before later working in Mum's bagel shop.

'What have you done?' he asked.

'I've had the biggest barbecue, and it's gone on for two days, and the place is just a wreck.'

He cleaned up the mess from that party and then moved in for a while to help me out. He'd help look after Danielle and keep the house clean, which allowed me to go out and play snooker. But the house never stayed clean for long. A few days later I'd be having another party and then another.

Between parties I'd go to see Mum in Holloway. That was horrible. It was bad enough visiting Dad in the nick, but I'd grown used to that. Going to visit Mum was a different matter. What is going on here? I would think when I saw her. She just didn't look right in prison. I looked at all the other women and they were big and butch, and then I looked at Mum and realised that she is quite a feminine lady. I wondered how she could deal with being inside. But she coped amazingly. She was always pleased to see me, and asked how Danielle was. I said everything was OK – I didn't want to tell her that I'd just had a party and smashed the house up, and that I'd been getting off my face. I'd get myself together before the visit so I could make out that everything was hunky-dory to stop her worrying.

After a few weeks of parties at the house and nightclubbing I was losing control. It was only when I went to Preston for the UK Championship and stayed in Liverpool with my mate Willy, aka the Yunzi, and his family, that I recovered a bit of stability. The best thing about going to Liverpool was that I asked Angie Chapman to look after Danielle. After the tournament I stayed up there and Angie continued to look after Danielle. I felt better knowing that Danielle was being well cared for, that the business was running as normal (Angie's son Gary was doing the banking), and that Mum and Dad's house was safely locked up in Chigwell.

I met the Yunzi via Dad. He was the best mate of Dad's mate Jimmy, from inside. Dad had asked me if I could sort some tickets out for the Yunzi, or Willy, as we then called him, for the UK Championship at Preston.

'He's a nice fella,' Dad said, 'he won't get in your way. He'll come and watch the snooker and he'll be gone.' I knew he must be someone special because whenever people asked Dad for tickets, he'd tell them to pay for their own and not to drive his boy mad because I already had enough on my plate.

'Dad, I won't let him down,' I said.

I phoned up Willy to tell him I'd sorted him a ticket. We were both in London, and agreed to meet at King's Cross and go down to Liverpool together. Dad told me, you'll know him when you see him because he's about 40 years old, he'll have a big smile on his face and he'll say, "Pleased to meet you".'

I was in the station, with my snooker cue and suitcase looking for this fella. He told me he'd be walking around the station at 7.30. I saw this big fella, and went up to him and said, 'You must be Willy.'

'Yeah,' he said, with a big smile. 'Pleased to meet you.'

We got on the train and chatted all the way there. We got a black cab to his house, put our bags down, and he said, 'Are you hungry?'

'Yeah, I'm starving.'

'Come on, we'll go and get a Chinese.'

Once I moved in with the Yunzi and his family I felt I was around people who did normal things – got up in the morning, did a day's work. When they went to work I'd go out and play snooker. We'd eat dinner and watch telly together and live as a family. I no longer felt that I always had to be out doing something to enjoy myself. I've always loved family. The family unit is still something I crave. Shortly before Mum went to prison I'd made friends with a fella called Benny who lived in Stanford-le-Hope, near Basildon. He had a lovely-looking daughter of about my age who I fancied like mad. I felt a bit funny asking her out because Benny was my mate, but eventually we got together. We became like a family. I'd stay over there (we slept in separate bedrooms), she'd bring me breakfast in bed, and we'd sit in the garden during the day and go out clubbing at night – all of us: me, my girlfriend, her dad and her mum. It was mental, but I loved it. My own family had become so screwed up, with Dad already in prison and Mum under investigation, and this became a surrogate family for me. It was such a lovely life – we'd spend all our time together, then we'd go down to the pub at 10 p.m., come back at 1 a.m., have a few drinks and a laugh. But soon after Mum went to jail Benny's daughter and I split up, and that's when I started to go off the rails. I was out of control, drinking and puffing like mad to make up for my lack of confidence. But the Yunzi came to my rescue.

It wasn't until I met him that I cut down on the drink and dope. But I had to find a substitute, and that substitute was food. I put on four stones in a few months. We'd eat five good meals a day, starting with a huge fry-up in the morning and carrying on like that through the day until we had a massive supper. Even then we weren't finished: at about 11 p.m. every night we'd wander off down the street for a Chinese. With the Yunzi, who was a food addict himself, to keep me company, I convinced myself that I had to be big; that it was good and healthy to be big. The few times I tried to lose some weight by going for a run, he'd look at me and say, 'You're fucking mad, Rock. You're running yourself into the ground.' So I'd go back to stuffing my face. I'd swapped one addiction for another.

I went to visit Mum in prison to tell her I was staying in Liverpool and Danielle was being looked after by Angie. Mum was relieved, I think, but she felt hopeless. She thought she'd deserted us, and tortured herself with the thought that she'd let her family down. Dad must be thinking the same thing, but Mum is much more logical and unforgiving – towards both herself and others. If Dad meets a fella with any good about him, he'll have a laugh and take him on board, whereas with Mum it'll be 'No, my family comes first.' I don't think she could bear the thought that Danielle was living with someone else and I had moved up north. While she worried that the family was falling apart, Dad was probably thinking, Well, he's 19, she's 12, she'll be all right with Angie, and if he ain't big enough and ugly enough to look after himself now, he never will be. I'm doing a bit of bird, she's doing a bit of bird, let's get on with it. That's Dad's philosophy all over – just crack on. When Mum hasn't seen me for a while she looks me up and down, asks if I've been eating all right, decides I haven't and that I need a bowl of pasta and to relax, whereas Dad is all 'Relax? Just get your finger out of your arse and sort yourself out.' Mum never told me how worried she was, but I always knew.

Whenever I asked Mum how she was, she always

told me she was having a right laugh inside, doing courses in food hygiene and keep-fit. The course in hygiene proved useful when we opened up a bagel shop later in Chingford, but really she felt useless in prison, in spite of getting into shape.

Someone else who took up keep-fit, amazingly, was the Yunzi. He's lost four or five stones, is running six miles three times a week, eating the right amounts of the right kinds of food, and has packed up smoking; all at the age of 47. When I saw him the other day he told me that for the first time in years he feels great. It was the first time I'd ever seen him able to cross his legs – it's mad the things you notice.

I love the Yunzi. He's like my second dad. My dad will always be my dad, and I'll always love him to bits, but I can't easily go to Dad with my problems when he's inside. Yes, I can speak to him on the phone, but there's only so much you can say like that. And there's only so much I want to tell him of my problems when he's in jail – I don't want to burden him with my worries when he's got so many of his own.

When I was at my most desperate the Yunzi was there for me. And he wasn't there for me because I had money, or because I was a snooker player, or because he wanted to be a hanger-on. I had plenty of hangers-on, and I know the difference between one of them and a genuine person. The Yunzi was a godsend for me because I was in a bad way. I stayed with him and his family on and off for eighteen months. I didn't want to come back to London at the time because I'd made so many friends, genuine people, up in Liverpool. I felt safe there. When I was in London I felt so vulnerable to the hangers-on, but in Liverpool the Yunzi and all his friends weren't people who wanted me to go on the piss with them all the time or wanted to exploit me in any way. They were just nice family people.

Mum got weekend leave six weeks before she was released and I picked her up and drove her home. She was sitting in the house, just looking round her, and she couldn't believe it. She was so pleased to be back. The next day she went to see Dad in prison, and then she had to be back at her prison for 8 p.m., otherwise she'd have got extra days for being late. It was the maddest rush of a weekend we'd ever had. I kissed her goodbye and Barry Hearn's driver, Robbo, drove her up to the prison to see Dad before taking her back to her prison. They almost didn't make it: Robbo had to drive like crazy down the hard shoulder to get her there on time. She arrived at 7.55 p.m. and I went back up to the Yunzi's. I was having a little puff in Liverpool every now and then, but I felt safe and stable with the family. My life was a mess, but I knew there were people around me to stop me treading over the line. The Yunzi's family watched me closely to make sure I didn't go too mad.

A month and a half later, when Mum came home, so did I. I met her at the prison, and it was great to be reunited. But not for long: about two weeks later she threw me out. I was soon back to my bad habits.

She said I was too fat, and she couldn't stand all the puffing and all the drinking.

Throughout the time she had been away, my snooker had been terrible. I won one tournament – the Charity Challenge – but most of the players weren't interested in it because it wasn't a ranking event. I played well, but even then I was in no fit state.

Somehow I made my way to the semi-finals of the World Championship, but it was just after I lost, at the end of the season in 1996, that Mum kicked me out. 'I can't stand this no more,' she said, 'watching you throw your life away. I'm embarrassed by you. Look at you. I want you to get your bags and go. Sort your life out. Do what you've got to do. But I don't want to see you doing it.'

'Fair enough,' I said.

I left home and moved into the Britannia Hotel in Docklands. I couldn't believe that she'd chucked me out, but thought, Fuck it, I'm on my own. I'm going to do what I really want to do now. I started getting into a bit of trouble. One night I had a fight in a pub: a few people started on me and I hit one of them, then some of them battered me with snooker cues. There were only about twenty people in the pub, but unfortunately they were all together. I heard one of them say, 'Do him, do him.' I was in serious trouble so I kicked off my shoes and ran.

A couple of weeks later Mum and I made up and I went back home.

I was almost sixteen stones at the time, and didn't

feel good about what I saw in the mirror. I had a thirty-seven-inch waist and kept having to go to tailors to have bigger waistcoats made. Then there was the dope: it slaughtered me. After I left Yunzi's, where I'd just had the occasional joint, I started smoking big time. I used to laugh at everything and think everyone else was mad, and that they ought to try some of this stuff because it took all the stress out of life. Clearly I'd lost my sense of reality. I'd sleep, smoke, eat, sleep, smoke, eat, sleep, smoke, eat. That was the routine of my life. I'd phone up minicab firms and say, 'I want you to get a cab driver to go up to McDonald's to get three hamburgers, two large fries, a large chocolate milkshake, nine nuggets, four ketchups and three barbecue sauces. And a large Diet Coke.' God knows why I bothered with the Diet Coke! A few minutes later there'd be a knock on the door and there'd be a massive carrier bag from McDonald's, and I'd eat and eat and eat. Then I'd have a joint and want to eat some more. I'd order enough Chinese for about five people because I knew I'd eat, fill myself up, have more joints, and then want to eat some more. I was turning into Elvis! Then in the middle of the night I'd wake up, get the munchies, run into the kitchen and start eating loads more food.

I lost track of the days and, of course, the snooker went out of the window. I'd go out to a club, get back really late, feel awful the next day, ring up a mate, go and watch telly, have a few joints and a few drinks, and then it would be evening again. We'd be sitting around playing cards, eating, smoking and drinking until 3 a.m. One day flowed into the next. Nothing seemed to matter any more.

I felt there was no way out of this: it was my life and I might as well make the most of it. But it wasn't a constant downhill slide. There was a switch in my head that flipped every so often and told me, 'Ronnie, you're dropping down the rankings.' I'd suddenly realise how fat I'd become and I'd go on a massive mission for three weeks: go down the gym every day, practise every day and stay away from all my mates who spent their life puffing. I'd get myself back in shape, but as soon as I did I'd go and see my old friends and start puffing again.

I was on the verge of falling out of the top sixteen. I went from three down to thirteen in the rankings in the 1995–6 season. It was only at the end of that season that I managed to pull myself up a bit by getting to the semi-finals of both the British Open and the World Championship. That pushed me back up to number eight.

In a way I was happy; well, happier. I didn't care so much about everything any more, but the flipside was that I didn't really care about anything. I'd given up on myself. I was fed up with trying to get my game and myself right. It seemed like too much effort. But I still knew enough to feel sad that my life had ended up like this. I had no discipline, no control, I couldn't say no, I needed people around me – not positive people, negative people. Positive people frightened the life out of me. That's why I stayed away from David Beckham – because he was so positive.

I first met him in a club called Charlie Chan's. It was during my binging period. I love football, and had always known he was something special. We had a couple of drinks and got on well. David was well known, but nothing like as famous as he is these days. As we left the club, I heard a girl say to her mate, 'Look, there's David Beckham!'

Her mate said, 'Which one? The fat one or the skinny one?'

I thought, Fuck me, I must be fat. And I was – I was enormous.

David told me to come and see him in Manchester, so I went up there and spent a few days with him. He's a lovely fella, and he was great to be around. But I couldn't cope with being around someone who was doing so well. I liked being around wasters because it made me feel better. Anyone who was doing well, like David or Michael Owen or Prince Naseem, made me feel worse about myself. In my eyes they were winners, and I looked at myself as a loser. I felt out of my depth. Unsurprisingly, David and I fell out of touch, which was a real shame.

Around this time I went to Vegas with a group of mates to watch the boxing. The football manager Graeme Souness was staying in our hotel and I got chatting to him about sport and life in general. 'Healthy body, healthy mind,' he said, which had always been my dad's philosophy, too. I knew he was right. No top sportsman is fat; they all keep themselves in shape. After speaking to Graeme I packed up smoking, both cigarettes and dope, and restricted myself to a few drinks a day. I was in the gym for two hours a day, three miles on the runner, twenty minutes on the bike, then another three miles. I had four months to get myself ready for the next season. I'm obsessive about everything. When I start practising snooker after the summer break I don't start at 10 a.m. and finish at 5 p.m., I play until ten at night, until I've got blisters on my hand. And if I go running, I'll go twice a day – in the morning and in the evening – and by the second run I'm flying; I've convinced myself I'm a triathlete, on the way to the Olympics. If I play golf, I have to go on a range, hit four hundred balls and then go and play a round afterwards because that's what Tiger Woods does. Tiger Woods is a role model for me: I'd love to achieve in snooker what he has already achieved in golf.

As I said, I'd got the fitness bug a few times in the past, but I'd never approached it as obsessively as I was now. I was down the gym for 7 a.m., breakfast, circuit training, lunch, then more circuit training. I was probably training four hours a day, every day, and I got so fit. Two months into it, I looked in the mirror and saw definition in my upper body for the first time. Amazing! I'd grown tits! That spurred me on even more. I took my diet seriously. Whereas previously I lived on McDonald's, now it was fish, potatoes, no butter, just a bit of bread (good carbohydrate), chicken for the protein, no red meat because it took hours to digest. I cut out alcohol completely because it was fattening, as well as a downer, and replaced it with all sorts of juices. The juicer was a godsend for me. I've never been one for going over to the fruit bowl and dipping in, but I love to make my own juices. I had a carrot, celery, apple and orange fruit juice this morning – lovely. It was like a meal. After about four months I'd lost more than four stones and was down to eleven stones. People thought I'd been taking special drugs or gone on a starvation diet because they reckoned there was no way I could lose so much weight so quickly without cheating. They couldn't believe it because I'd looked such a slob the season before and I'd lost all the weight in the close season. But the people who thought that obviously don't know me very well. I've never been one for diets. I eat because I'm happy and am enjoying my food, *and* I eat because I'm miserable for comfort. I love eating, whatever. The difference was that I'd started eating healthily and training like crazy. I wanted to do it for myself and for the snooker – there was no way I could play at my best when I was so grossly over-weight. And I had started to feel bad about my shape. People would pat my belly and make remarks about my size, and it felt like when I'd been doing football training all those years ago and the kids took the piss out of me for not being able to do press-ups and called me fatty.

At one point I even thought about going off to college and becoming a keep-fit instructor. I used to look at keep-fit instructors and think, They're 40 and they're looking great. I want some of that when I'm 40. I might still do it when I finish playing snooker. I think if I hang around fit people their habits will rub off on me. If I hang around with people who drink and take drugs their habits rub off on me. So my theory is that if I want to achieve something, or change my life in some way, I need to hang around with the right people. If I want to be a professional golfer, which I do one day, I need to hang around with the best golfers in the world – go on a tour, blend in, pick up useful tips, and then you can't go wrong if you're learning off the best.

My snooker picked up massively when I got fit. I felt alert, and even though I'd not done much of a spiritual job on my inside, I looked all right on the outside, which was a good start.

My priority now was to win tournaments. I went to Thailand and won the first ranking event of the 1996–7 season. I was well chuffed, but in the next tournament, the Grand Prix, I lost in the second round. By then I'd started going out again and was back puffing.

It was time for the UK Championship – the second-biggest tournament in snooker. I was still looking good, and everybody was telling me so, and I'd got some self-respect back. I was drawn against Terry Murphy, who I'd only played once before, when I was a kid. I must have been 13 or 14, and I beat him in a Pro-Am. He was about 19 at the time, and I'd been told he was a good player, but when it came to the match I just battered him. It was eight years on now, and he'd not really done anything on the pro circuit. I went into the match thinking, I'll just find my feet and once I start cueing well he's got no chance.

I went 3–1 down and started to panic. I thought, I'm playing shit and there is no way out of this. Mentally, I was all over the place; I didn't know what day it was. I came out after the interval and I didn't pot a ball: 3–1 became 4–1; 4–1 became 5–1; then 6–1; and 7–1. It was the first to nine frames and I was 7–1 down. I was thinking, Jesus Christ, what has gone on here? This is a nightmare, get me out of here. I was awful and he was playing like God against me. Every time I missed he punished me. He was potting balls from everywhere and never looked as if he were going to miss.

We weren't due back on the table until the next evening. Basically, I'd lost. There was no way I could come back from 7–1, not the way Terry was playing. But I was hitting a few balls with my coach and helper Del next day and all of a sudden the game became easy again. I was hitting the cue ball so sweetly. I hadn't felt that good since I was 16, in the first year of qualifying for the World Championship in Blackpool. This was the moment I'd been waiting five years for. I'd been desperate all this time to recapture that buzz. I knew it was in there some-where and I wanted it to come out so badly. I was only practising, but suddenly all the years of frus-tration were gone. I was certain I was going to win not only the match, but the whole tournament.

'I tell you what,' I said to Del, 'I'm going to win this match. I'm going to win this match, and you know what, I'm going to win the tournament.'

'I know. You're hitting the ball like a dream,' Del said.

I met Del back in 1992 at Blackpool. He came up to me, after I'd just thrashed Graham Crispsy 5–0, and said, 'I've never seen anyone play like you, Ron.' We became mates. He turned up at tournaments over the next couple of years and by 1996 he had become my coach – not exactly a professional snooker coach, but more a Mr Motivator.

When I start playing well I turn into the ReadyBrek kid – I'm glowing, floating. And this is what was happening. I skipped back to the hotel, and I couldn't wait to put on my suit and go out there and play, because I knew I was going to have so much fun. And that's what happened. I went out there and won three frames with a 90, an 80 and a century. The score was now 7–4 and it was the last frame before the twenty-minute interval. I missed a blue that I should have potted, and Terry went 8–4 up. On one level I wasn't happy: I'd wanted 7–5, which was a huge difference to 8–4. But on another level I was ecstatic and still fancied I could win it.

But that meant I'd have to win the next five frames. I got it back to 8–6, and he missed a chance in the next frame. I started talking to him. I know it's not right to do that, but I couldn't help myself. 'The old pressure's getting you there?' It was 8–7 and I was two frames away from pulling off the best result of my life. I'd beaten Stephen Hendry, John Higgins, Mark Williams and Matthew Stevens, all of them much better players, but this would have been the biggest of the lot. I made a break of 20 and then fell out of position, but I played a good safety shot and I was praying he'd go for the red. If he missed I was in for 8–8 and I'd have him by the bollocks. I was on the edge of my chair, waiting to jump up. I was watching him closely and his arm was shaking. There seemed to be no way he could pot it. But he did, and went on to make 67. I needed two or three snookers. I tried for them but it was never going to happen, and when he potted a red I had to shake his hand. It was all over. 'Well played,' I said.

We did the interviews afterwards, and he was slumped, exhausted, supping a pint of lager, trying to revive himself.

'I nearly had you,' I said. 'You know it, don't you? You did well, but I nearly had you. I was on you.' And I felt happy – I'd been beaten, but I put in a performance that I enjoyed, and I know the crowd enjoyed. I know Terry didn't enjoy it because no one enjoys someone coming at you like that. But all credit to him: that 67 was the best break under pressure anyone has ever made against me. Admittedly, Stephen Hendry once got a 147 in the final frame against me – but that was in a charity event.

I was in the car coming back with Del, and I said to him, 'I'm going to win the next tournament.' Because I'd been beaten in the first round, I had two

weeks to practise before the German Open. I knew
that if I went there with the same form there was no
way I could lose. I would have bet my life on it. The
only nagging thought in my mind was that it was
too good to last. I'd not played this well for five
years: I was making ten or eleven centuries every day
at the practice table. I felt I was back – I felt buzzy,
I didn't need a drink, didn't need a drug, didn't need
to do anything self-destructive. In Germany I won
my first match 5–1, and then beat Stephen Hendry
5–2. He'd just won the UK Championship so he
was full of confidence, and I caned him. I beat Nigel
Bond 6–1 in the semis, with breaks of 141, 144, 138.
He came off the table and said, 'I can't believe
that.'

I was in the final against Alain Robidoux. Six
months earlier I'd had a row with him. He had
claimed that I hadn't shaken his hand before the final
session of a match at Sheffield. The score was 7–2
and I'd been out on the town the previous night till
about 6 a.m. My mate had to give me a piggyback
upstairs, and as he did I was spewing all over the
hotel corridors. Lovely. He threw me in bed. Next
day they got me up in the afternoon and threw me
in the steamer to liven me up a bit. I only needed to
win three frames against Robidoux, which I
managed. In one of the frames I started playing a
few left-handed shots. I'd been practising it because
it makes life so much easier if you can play some
shots left-handed.

At the end, it was Robidoux who wouldn't shake

my hand. He just walked out of the arena and I was left in the middle of the Crucible Theatre. The audience was as baffled as I was. First, I was told that he didn't shake my hand because I hadn't shaken his at the start of the session, and he thought I was trying to psyche him out. I certainly couldn't remember not shaking his hand. 'Are you sure?' I said. But then it came out: 'Oh, and he didn't like the left-handed business either.' He was standing right at the end of the corridor when I was doing my interview, so he could hear me. 'I'll play him again,' I said, 'and I'll play him left-handed and I'll beat him because he is no good.' It wasn't the most diplomatic thing I've ever said, but I was thinking, Right, if you want to start playing games, I'll have some games with you.

In the final of the German not surprisingly there was a sense of unfinished business. Having said that, Alain was a good sport and was just glad to be in the final, irrespective of who he was playing. I went 7–3 up and was looking pretty comfortable, but I wasn't playing as well as I had been earlier in the week. And then my form, and my head, went altogether. For a month the cue had felt like part of my body and everything seemed so easy. Then suddenly it wasn't there. I was no longer interested in winning the match. I just thought, Oh, here we go again, the bad form's back for another five years. He clawed one frame back, then three more to make it 7–7. He was 40-odd in front and at the table with 59 left on, but he missed. I got out of my chair and did a clearance to go 8–7 up. Then I won the final frame with a hundred break.

I'd won, but my mind was playing tricks with me again. I was preoccupied with playing badly instead of thinking, I'm 7–3 up and not playing well, what could be better? That's the attitude I have now. A bit of silverware is a bit of silverware, however it's won – worry about the form later. I've got much more faith in my ability now.

Because I felt good in myself, in how I looked, I thought it wouldn't hurt to have a little puff, so I started smoking again. And I started getting back into the habit of hanging around people who took drugs. But I combined it with the fitness regime and that held me together for a while. I could go out, have a good night of it, and get up first thing in the morning and run it off. After six or seven miles I was ready for the day.

But it didn't last. I started to train less and go clubbing. I was trying to convince myself I was in control and reasoned that if I did pile on the weight again, all I needed to do was another four months' solid training, just like last time. But it wasn't as easy as that.

CHAPTER SIX

Off the Rails

When as a kid I saw Mum and Dad going out and having a good time, I knew they could do it because they'd done well for themselves. So, to me, it became a symbol of success. One day, I thought, when I'm successful I'll be doing the nightclubs. I also equated a certain attitude with success. I would look at the young kids who'd made it – films stars and pop stars – and so often they were loud, rude and arrogant. And soon enough that's what I became. I was obnoxious. I was the new kid on the block, and thought I could do as I liked. These were my 'Liam Gallagher' days. I bought into that idea that I had to be a bad boy, that I was the third Gallagher brother (strictly speaking the fourth, but you know what I mean) and that wherever I went I had to cause trouble. And if I didn't, I was letting down my reputation.

I looked up to the Gallagher brothers. They were just making it big at the time and I'd read that they were always in fights or telling people to fuck off. Fair enough where Liam is concerned, but I've met Noel, and he's not at all aggressive. He said to me, 'I get people telling me that you look like me.'

'*I* get told I look like you, too,' I said. Unfortunately, I'd much rather look like Liam. I never mentioned that to Noel.

We were pissed, and had had a bit of the other stuff, too, and we chatted for two hours. I must have bored the pants off him. It was at a celebrity party – the most mental party I've been to in my life – at Dungeons. Everyone was there – Mick Jagger, Ronnie Wood, Jools Holland, Kate Moss and Noel. It was one of the best nights of my life. It was a fancy-dress party, but I didn't want to look like an idiot, so I just turned up in jeans and a T-shirt with Jimmy White and David Gray (the snooker player, not the singer). I had to play Jimmy two days later in the Champions Cup. When we got to Dungeons the place was heaving, hot and sweaty, and Jimmy didn't want to stay too long. The booze was flowing, the music was loud and the place was a riot. I told him not to be silly, the party was wonderful. 'Come on, Jimmy!' I said. 'Relax, chill out, we'll have a good night. I'm playing you on Sunday so I'm in the same boat.' Despite what I was saying, both of us knew we shouldn't be there. Then I thought, Fuck it. How often do you get to party with Mick Jagger?

Jimmy eventually left but I'd had a few drinks by then and didn't even notice that he'd gone. So I was on my own with David Gray, and feeling a bit shy because I didn't know people too well. We just sat at the bar and drank and quietly star spotted, until I noticed Noel Gallagher. I shouted, 'Noel!' and he looked round but he couldn't see who had called him, and I lost the bottle, and didn't say anything.

Then as he came back I shouted out again, 'Noel!' And he went, 'All right, mate,' and came over and started chatting. I think his then wife Meg was pregnant at the time. I spent ages asking him what his brother was like, telling him how much I loved his music, all that sort of crap. Then, out of nowhere, he asked, 'How much are you worth?' Fucking hell, I thought, what sort of question is that to ask? Dad had told me never ask anyone what they do for a living, and never ask anyone how much they're worth. It seemed such a weird thing to ask when we were having a chat and a laugh, and we hardly knew each other. And when somebody's worth £100 million, unless you've got at least £30 million yourself you're going to feel a bit pathetic, aren't you? So I laughed off the question.

After a couple of hours he said he had to go because his wife Meg wasn't feeling too good, and true enough she did look quite miserable. We swapped numbers, and I phoned him once, left a number on the answer machine. He never got back to me, so I thought, I'm not going to drive him mad, he must have so many people on his case, and I let it be. But he was a right nice fella – despite asking what I was worth.

Ronnie Wood, who I'd met a couple of times before, came up to me a bit later. 'Hey, you're playing Jimmy on Sunday ain't ya?'

'Yeah,' I said, 'he's got no chance. He needs to go to bed at eleven at night. I'll give him a good hiding.'

At 4 a.m., I went off with Ronnie's son, Jamie. He

and his mates had a couple of rooms booked at the Grosvenor. I remember looking out of the window and thinking, How come it's daylight out there. When I'm out I never want it to end, but I felt like shit that morning. And at the back of my mind I knew I had to show up the next day for the match against Jimmy. It was 9 a.m. by now, and David Gray and I went back to my mate's house, had a couple of hours' kip, and then went back home.

Mum looked at me and saw the state I was in. 'You all right?' she said. But she knew I wasn't.

'I've got to go,' I said, 'because I've booked a hotel and have to do an interview.'

She knew I'd been on a bender, especially when she saw David in the suit that he'd been wearing the night before.

David's a good player. He wasn't at the time, but now he's number seventeen in the world. It's only since he's stopped hanging around with me and Jimmy that he's improved so much! He came down to Croydon with me, we checked in to the hotel and I slept from five in the evening right through till nine the next morning. I was due to play Jimmy at 11 a.m.

It was the worst match ever shown on British TV. People came up to me afterwards and said, 'That was such bad snooker we thought it was fixed.' And those were the highlights! In the first frame I got to the table and made 4, Jimmy made 10, I made 6, Jimmy made 12, I made 18. I won the frame with a 22 clearance on the black. It took me two frames even to begin to come round. I ended up winning the match 4–2. Jimmy must have been sick. Or maybe it *was* true what I'd said to Ronnie Wood about Jimmy needing to be in bed by eleven every night.

Ronnie Wood's got a snooker room at his house in Kingston, and Jimmy and I have played some of our finest snooker there. I've only met Keith Richards a couple of times, but he's one of the nicest fellas I've ever known, which came as a surprise after all the stories I'd heard. Once I was round at Ronnie's with Jimmy and there was a guitar there with a huge hole in it.

'See this guitar?' said Ronnie.

'Yeah.'

'Keith was playing it and I told him it was Mick's. He said, "Fuck, I never play Mick's guitar," and he put a pillow over it and shot it!'

There were loads of pillow feathers stuck in it so I'm sure the story was true. After hearing this, I thought, When I meet this geezer I'd better be careful what I say: polite and nice, 'Yes Keith, no Keith,' just keep the peace.

That night we had arrived at Ronnie's at about 3 a.m. after playing an exhibition match in Blackburn. It was pissing down with rain. Jimmy and I were still in our dinner suits, somewhat the worse for wear and talking a load of crap to each other. We were telling each other what we were going to do in the coming season – if we managed to get our heads straight – but we were really just a couple of lunatics waiting for the next party. I knew I could go round to Ronnie's at any time, knock on the door and just stay the night there. By the time we arrived, Ronnie's missus Jo had been asleep for hours. We stayed up till 6 a.m. just playing snooker – me, Jimmy and Ronnie. He's got the best snooker room I've seen in my life: the ceiling is as high as you can see, the settees are unbelievably comfortable. Ronnie's not a bad player – he can make 20 breaks – and he loves the game. It's his dream to make a century break, and I've tried to give him lessons, but it's difficult because I don't really know how I do it myself.

Eventually, once it was daylight, I went to bed. The room was full of bottles and glasses, a right mess, and I said to Ronnie, 'I've got to help tidy this up.' He said, 'Don't worry, just get off to bed.'

I got up at lunchtime, went downstairs, and the place was spotless. I said to Ronnie, 'Blimey, Jo don't hang about, she's fantastic.'

'Nah!' he said. 'We had the cleaners come in. We don't do none of that.'

The cleaners would turn up about 10 a.m., Ronnie would still be in bed, they'd let themselves in, tidy up and leave.

Next day, Keith Richards was there. We had a few drinks and ended up in the snooker room. Ronnie said, 'I want you to show Keith how you play snooker.' So Jimmy and I played eleven frames – he had six centuries, and I had five. It was the best I'd ever played, and it was probably the best Jimmy's ever played. I got more of a buzz out of that than winning the World Championship – and God knows I got a big enough buzz from that! Keith said, 'This is like Mozart.' And I know Mozart, I've watched *Amadeus*, and to me that was a massive compliment. After every frame, Jimmy and I couldn't wait to set up the balls for the next one. Eleven frames, eleven centuries. We were off our nuts. Keith was standing there with a big jug of vodka and orange, and it was like fuel for us. Every fifteen minutes he'd come back with the jug refilled for me and Jimmy. Even if we'd not been playing so brilliantly, the state we were in we would have *thought* we were.

We ended up going to Wimbledon dogs that night with Ronnie, Jo, Keith and his missus Pam, and Ronnie's manager. I love the dogs – it's always full of duckers and divers. I met this fella there who I knew, a tipster, and he kept telling me what to back. And I won on every race – I walked out with about a thousand quid.

Another time we went on a massive bender, eventually ending up in a classy Fulham restaurant for Ronnie's mum's birthday. I think it was her 80th, and all of Ronnie's family were there. We sat there for two or three hours, but were in no state to eat a thing. Then we went off to Ronnie's brother's house. Around 4 a.m. we headed off back to Ronnie's and carried on till eight. We'd been going two days now. We'd drunk so much we were almost sober.

I woke up the next morning, thought, Enough's enough, better go home, and told Ronnie I was leaving.

'No,' he croaked, 'I want you to stay.' Typical

Ronnie. He hates the end of a party every bit as much as I do.

They were the good days. But so many of the days I had out were anything but good. I was keeping a lot of bad company, had loads of hangers-on. In London I found I could pick up hangers-on anywhere. I picked up two on a train coming back from a tournament. They were from Scotland and I asked them what they were planning to do down in London.

'Nothing. Do you recommend anything?'

'Yeah,' I said, 'come to the Emporium.'

They said they had to dump their suitcases at the hotel first, and then they'd come down.

'No,' I said, 'don't bother with that, we'll go straight to Soho and you can put your bags in one of my shops.' So we went to Brewer Street, got there about midnight, asked the staff to look after the bags in one of the sex shops, and told them we'd come and get them the next day.

We stayed at the Emporium till five in the morning. I'd never met these people before. I think if they'd not recognised me they would have thought I was going to mug them, but because they knew my face they felt safe. I suppose I just wanted company. I didn't want to go home to bed. I wanted to go out and pull birds and take drugs. I didn't have any mates I could rely on in London at the time, and these two strangers were as good to hang around with as anyone else. I'd always been like that; always done things on the spur of the moment. I could see some 'mates' on the street at midday and that could be the start of a cycle for three days. I wouldn't go home and get changed, no matter how scruffy I looked; I'd just be out punishing my credit card.

Once, I'd just bought a brand-new BMW, and we were so pissed, on such a mission, that my mate pulled out of my drive and smashed up the car.

'Don't worry about that,' I said, 'let's just worry about where we've got to go.'

That was the nuttiness of it – I didn't even care that somebody had just smashed up my car. It wasn't important. It was just a machine that got us from A to B and looked good. I thought I could do whatever I liked and get away with it. But I couldn't.

I wanted to be raw like an animal. Not for me sitting in a Chelsea coffee shop with my shades on, looking cool and sophisticated. My attitude worked with the birds when I was sober, but whenever I got tipsy I could be aggressive and not surprisingly they steered clear of me. I had my fair share of girls, but not many lasted. I had only three or four serious girlfriends; but I had plenty of not-so-serious ones. When I was 17 and 18, I'd have about ten on the go at once – French girls, Romanian girls. Most of them were regulars on the snooker circuit. Everywhere I went I had to have a bird on the go. We'd meet them in lapdancing gaffs and take them out.

I was tagged as a bad boy from the early days – partly because of the way I played and partly because of my family's history. Right from the start of my professional life it was 'Ronnie O'Sullivan, whose father is inside.' Then there was the fact that Mum also went inside, so they always assumed I must have been up to a bit of the naughty stuff.

Mind you, they often had a point. The first bit of trouble I got into was when I smashed up a motor in the driveway of a hotel I was staying at in Blackpool. I'd been doing 60 m.p.h. – you were only supposed to do 15 m.p.h. – going over speed humps, and they had three together in rapid succession to make sure you slowed down good and proper in time for a roundabout. I hit the first one and the second, and by the third I was out of control. I had four girls in the car with me, and behind us my mates were in a taxi with another couple of girls. I smashed the motor into the sign in the centre of the roundabout, which said, 'Welcome to the Village Hotel'. When the car came to a stop one girl was under the dashboard, and the other three were cowering in the back. I remember asking if everyone was all right, checking to make sure nobody had lost any arms or legs. Then I said, 'Right, let's get out of the car and go and have a drink.' The car, a BMW 325, was smashed to bits. This was just after I won the UK in 1993. I was only 17. A couple of years later I was banned for a year for driving 133 m.p.h. down the M3.

I'd always had a thing for motors. Just the other day Dad reminded me of the time I decided to take Mum's thirty-five-grand BMW for a ride. I was 13 at the time. I was just going down the road when he passed me on his way home. He says he tried to keep calm because he didn't want to scare me, but really he wanted to knock my block off.

I used to drive Mum's motor up and down the driveway. Mum knew about it, but she trusted me, and said, 'Ron, don't be silly, don't try to take it anywhere.' One day I thought, I'm out of here. I drove round the block and brought it back, parked it and thought Mum wouldn't notice. And she didn't. Lovely! So next day I took it out and thought, I'll go down to my mate's, which was about a mile away. So I was driving down the main road and I saw this familiar car coming towards me. Mum's BMW had all the trimmings – there wasn't another one like it around our way – and I knew I had to stop because there was no way Dad would miss me.

'Where you going, Son? Just for a drive down the Street?' he said when I pulled over.

'Nah, I'm off to see my mates.'

'Take the car home,' he said. 'I'll see you back there in a minute.' That's when he decided he had to take me in hand.

I drove it home, shitting myself the whole way. I got such a bollocking that I never took their cars out again.

The maddest incident of all was being pulled in for abduction in 1994. I was staying at a health farm in Hertfordshire, Hanbury Manor, after Dennis Taylor had beaten me in the Benson and Hedges. Everybody was asking what was wrong with my game – I'd just won the UK Championship so I was expected to beat Dennis easily, but he ended up pumping me 5–1. I didn't know what had gone wrong, but it certainly wasn't lack of practice. I'd been practising seven or eight hours every day, and if anything I might have overdone it. I thought I needed a break, so I said to my mate Jamie Fox, 'Do you fancy going to Hanbury Manor?'

So we booked in the hotel for a week of chilling out. We ate healthy food, didn't go out anywhere for a couple of days, just played golf, swam, worked out in the gym and chilled. At the end of the week Barry Hearn was promoting a fight in Brentwood, which is just down the road, so we arranged to meet a few mates, went to watch the boxing, and then drove to a Chinese restaurant for a bit to eat. By then, it was about one in the morning. We finished our meal, dropped a couple of mates off, and I was left with Jamie and another friend. Suddenly police converged on us from all sides. I didn't have a clue what was going on, but I knew it couldn't have anything to do with me. I was surprised enough when one of the officers walked up to my car, but I was gobsmacked when he ordered us out, threw me in the meat wagon, threw Jamie in one police car and our mate in the other, and took us all to separate police stations.

In the meat wagon they said they were arresting me for abduction. I didn't even know what that was.

'Hold on a minute,' I said. 'Can you please tell me what abduction is?'

'Kidnapping,' they said.

'You're having a laugh, aren't you?' I said.

The plainclothes officer, who was dressed in a suit,

obviously wasn't having any sort of a laugh.

I said, 'No comment' to everything, just as my dad had taught me.

They drove me down to the station, put me in a cell, took all my clothes off me and gave me a white paper suit to wear. All the officers were milling around because they'd heard they'd got a snooker player in. They asked me if I wanted a solicitor, but I couldn't get through to my lawyer so I had to use one that they had.

I was baffled by what was happening, but at least I knew it was all complete rubbish. Every couple of hours they took me up for more interviewing, but each time I said I had nothing to say. Then I was taken back down again. They wouldn't let me phone Mum to sort out the lawyer, saying that I wasn't allowed to make contact with anyone from outside, but by about 10 a.m. Mum had found out what was going on. She came down to the station and brought me some food.

The police gradually explained to me what I was supposed to have done. They told me my car had been reported as driving erratically through Chigwell with three passengers – which was probably correct because I did drive like a lunatic in the early days. Ten minutes later, someone went to another nearby police station and reported that a woman had been seen being dragged into a car with four people in it. They put one and one together and got three: they decided it must have been me who had abducted the woman.

But their times never added up. I was at the fight all night. There'd even been a TV camera there, so I told the police to ring Eurosport to get their video footage and it would prove that I was at the boxing at the time when the woman was pulled into the car.

At around 5 p.m. they let me go without charging me.

I never received an apology from the police. And the next day in the *Sun* there was a story headlined, SNOOKER ACE ON ABDUCTION CHARGE. At the end, they had a single sentence saying I was let off without being charged. It was at that point that I started thinking there was something going on. To me, the police seemed to have an agenda, seemed to be targeting us. It was about a year later that Mum was nicked, having been under surveillance for all that time.

For a couple of years I rarely seemed to be out of the news – for all the wrong reasons. Every month there seemed to be a story in the paper about the latest scrape I'd got into. Once I smashed the car and told my mate, 'That's OK because I'm getting a new one tomorrow.' It was a joke, but sure enough, next day in the paper the headline said, 36 GRAND CAR DOESN'T MATTER – RONNIE. HE'S GOING TO BUY A NEW ONE ANYWAY. It came out as if I were such a flash Jack the Lad.

Sometimes girls sold their stories to the *Sun*. Once I was a guest on *Big Break* and there was a story saying I was late on the show because I'd been having sex in the dressing room between rehearsals with one of the contestants. It was a fair cop.

Even years later the tabloids couldn't resist plastering me over their pages, when there was a bird, or maybe more than one, involved. In 2000 I was done for drink-driving with three girls, one of them in a dressing-gown. It wasn't nearly as saucy as it sounded. I'd been up in the West End with my girlfriend at the time, Bianca, and we were driving back. We were stopped at traffic lights when two girls pulled up alongside us and said, 'Ooh, nice car!' We were just chatting away, the lights turned green and I sped away in front of them. The police pulled me over. It was about 2 a.m. and there had been a Tube strike that night, so there were more than a hundred people standing outside Stratford station. Here we go, I thought, I'm going to be caught out again. All I could hear was people saying, 'It's Ronnie O'Sullivan,' and someone had a camera on them. Sure enough, it was in the paper next day – 'Ronnie caught driving with three girls.' Of course, they made a point of the fact that one of the girls in the other car was wearing a dressing-gown, and the other 'looked like a page 3 model'. I didn't even have a clue who these girls were.

I tried to give a sample at the police station, but the machine had broken down. They said they had a doctor coming down and he could sort it.

'He's not going to use a needle, is he?'

'Yes,' they said.

'Well, I don't do needles. I've got a phobia.'

'Well, that's for the doctor to decide when he comes down.'

'Fair enough, I'll explain it to the doctor, but nobody's sticking a needle in my arm.'

I ended up falling asleep on the couch in the station for a while. They kept me there for hours, and the last thing I wanted to do was get locked into a conversation with the police. I wish they had just put me in a cell and told me when they wanted me. I was finally given an hour to have a wee but I couldn't produce a sample. My lawyer explained to the police why I couldn't manage it. I'd been diagnosed as a depressive and had already started taking anti-depressants. The stress and tension left me unable to wee to order.

I was advised that it would save a lot of money and hassle to send in my licence and accept a ban – I was told that I'd get between a year and eighteen months. I was about to do that when my mate Mickey the Mullett said, 'Nah, can't have that. I've got the best person for you: Nick Freeman, he's a lawyer from Manchester and he's the bollocks. He could get Stevie Wonder a driving licence.' Nick was brilliant, and I got to keep my licence.

In 1996 I got done for headbutting the referee Len Ganley's son at the World Championship. Len and I had never got on well. I always felt that he often called misses against me, even though I never deliberately miss a ball – it's not my game. The missed ball is, in my opinion, one of the flawed rules of snooker. Len Ganley once came up to me at Blackpool and said,

'What's your dad's favourite meal? A carvery?' I just thought, you bastard. He comes across on telly as this jovial bloke, but he's nothing like that and he isn't well liked. He thought he was being funny when he said that about Dad. I tried to let it go over my head. I was 16 years old and things didn't bother me so much then because I was mentally strong, even though I didn't realise it at the time. Perhaps you have to crack up before you appreciate the strength you once had. Five years later I couldn't have dealt with it. If he had said that to me when I was 21, I would have wanted to smack him in the face.

I had even bigger problems with his son, Mike, which resulted in a thirty-grand fine and a suspended two-year ban. Mike Ganley was the Assistant Press Officer at the World Championship and was telling Del to get out of the players' lounge because he was wearing jeans. I said, 'Look, I'm just getting a couple of drinks and we're having dinner next door. We'll be off in a minute.'

'Nope. Now. Must go,' he said.

'Oh, fuck off,' I said.

He wouldn't drop it. Eventually I got him outside and nutted him. Then, when he was on the phone telling the tournament organiser Anne Yates what had happened, I said, 'Go on, you fucking grass,' and grabbed him by the nuts. Then I did a runner. I thought, I'd better get out of here before it all kicks off. I'd never headbutted anybody before and never have since. It's not really in me and I wasn't pleased that I had done it.

I thought Anne Yates might come to my rescue, but she came to find me and said, 'You're in trouble, you are.' They were going to throw me out of the World Championship because of the headbutting incident and I had to get my lawyer to sort it out. I was due to play John Higgins in the quarter-finals, but I didn't know whether they were going to let me continue. They had a disciplinary meeting, and I had to go up in front of the three board members. I think if it hadn't been for Jimmy Chambers (who knew me from when I was a kid) sticking up for me, I would have definitely been chucked out of the tournament. As it was, I was allowed to carry on and eventually lost to Peter Ebdon in the semis.

Just after that match Mum told me Sally was pregnant. Sally had been my on and off girlfriend for about a year, but we'd split up for good by the time I got the news. Oh fuck, I thought. It certainly hadn't been planned, and our relationship had always been pretty casual, but Sally had decided she wanted to go ahead and have the baby. I didn't know what to do – or what I was supposed to do. I was already depressed, and I didn't want to – or I couldn't – deal with this. She had the baby, called her Taylor, and I started paying her maintenance.

Pretty soon they moved away. I was giving them money each week and had bought them a house so they could get on with their lives, but for the first four years of Taylor's life I had nothing to do with her. It was only when I went into the Priory and I started to clear out my system that I began to think about what it meant to be a dad. When I came out of the Priory I wrote to Sally saying I'd like to see Taylor. She wrote back, 'I don't really want you to, because I know what you're like. You'll come and you'll go and it's not good for her.' I understood what she was saying and thought it was fair enough, but then I persisted and started spending a bit of time at their house. I was mad for Taylor when I saw her, and got so excited just watching her. I could see little bits of me in her – just like me she won't be told how to do anything. But I felt uncomfortable knowing that I wasn't really wanted there. I decided to let go, wait till Taylor's a little older and has got a mind of her own. Since then she has come to my house a few times. She is a beautiful little girl. I'm sad that I don't see more of her, but it just isn't meant to be at the moment. I'm sure we'll get to know each other better in the future.

Of all the incidents, the one that upset me most happened at the Irish Masters in March 1998. Jimmy White and I were out every night in Ireland. I'd just beaten him in the Masters, but he had to stay on for the Irish Bensons. I was being half-sensible because I was still in a big competition. We went down to Lilly Bordellos every night, but I just drank Guinness.

One night someone had a bit of puff cake. I'd never tried it. 'It's brilliant,' they said. So I took a bit and it gave me the giggles and I was buzzing. It was a bad decision. I'd not been playing well, but I had a feeling that my name was written on this trophy.

I'd had hard draws – Jimmy, then Stephen Hendry and John Higgins – but I still had a feeling that I would come through, and I did, beating Ken Doherty in the final. I didn't think in a million years that a bit of puff cake would show up in a drugs test, so when I was tested after the final I wasn't too bothered.

A few weeks later, Ian Doyle, who was managing me by then, came up to me during the World Championship and said, 'I need to have a word with you, it's very serious.'

'What is it?' I said.

'Just go to my room, I'll be there in about five minutes.'

I went to his room. When he turned up I asked, 'What's the matter?'

'They're saying that you've been caught with dope in you. You've failed a drugs test.'

'Oh, fuck!'

This was at the quarter-final stage of the World Championship.

'Don't worry about it,' said Ian, 'just get on and play your snooker.'

'Don't fucking worry about it? What's going to happen?'

I thought I might be banned. So I had that hanging over me when I went out to play John Higgins in the semis. I think it would have been better to wait until after the Worlds to tell me about it. Ian told me they would be doing the B sample after the Worlds, but as soon as I found out that I'd failed the first sample, I knew that was it.

I had to go in front of the disciplinary board after the second test came back positive. I said my piece, and they said they were going to think about it and would call me back in an hour. After lunch, they told me I was being stripped of the Irish Masters title and the money would go to Ken Doherty. Fair enough, I thought. I was quite happy at the time because at least I hadn't been banned. But then it sunk in and I was gutted. It was a lot of money – sixty grand – plus the trophy, both of which went to Ken.

In 2001 I won the Irish Masters again, and a journalist asked me how it felt to have finally won it for the first time.

'Hold on a minute,' I said. 'You better retract that question. This is the second time I've won it, the second time I've picked up the trophy. If you think a joint enhanced my performance, you must be dreaming. I won that tournament fair and square. If anything, it's done me a favour giving up the gear because it's the opposite of a performance enhancer. I've won this twice – get it right.' The journalist laughed.

Ken never won that tournament. If you ask him, he'll tell you he got blitzed in the final 9–3 in front of his home crowd.

I suppose in some ways I have deserved the bad boy tag, but I never felt I was a bad boy inside – never felt it was my true self. Hopefully, I'm going some way to losing that tag, but I don't think it will ever completely disappear. Perhaps it wouldn't be such a great thing if it did. After all, look through snooker history and, for some reason, it tends to be the bad boys with the talent who have been the most loved players in the game.

CHAPTER SEVEN

Facing Up to My Addiction

It may seem small to other people, but it's a huge part of my life. And I hate it: I can go a month totally clean and then I'll have to take a puff or a drink. I'm an addict struggling against my addictions and that's never going to change. I have an addictive personality. My addiction can be to anything. On a good day, it's snooker. On a bad day, it's drugs. My biggest thing has been cannabis. People tell you that you can't be a dope addict; that it's not addictive. I know differently.

It was 1998. I was back puffing and drinking, and heading for disaster. I was in pieces. I knew I needed help. I was a successful snooker player, back up to number three in the world, but I was miserable as sin. Part of my addictive personality is striving for perfection, and because I never achieved it, I constantly felt a sense of failure. It had been the pattern of my life for six or seven years: strive for perfection, fail to achieve it, despair. The strange thing was that I was comfortable being miserable. Whenever I was miserable I was quite happy, if that makes any sense. I was used to being in that position, and I had an excuse to shut people out, and get pissed or stoned.

What made me most uncomfortable was when I felt I had no right to be depressed. The classic occasion was when I beat John Higgins in his own back yard in Scotland to take the 1998 Embassy Masters. The maddest thing was that I even contemplated throwing the final because I knew after every Embassy tournament there was a big banquet where the sponsor's guests turn up with their programmes and the finalists sign them. I thought, Well, if I lose, I'll get loads of sympathy and can say, 'Yes, I'm gutted', and in a weird way I'll be happy with that. This was going through my mind as I was playing. I was tormenting myself, asking, Why do you want to throw away thirty thousand quid so you've got an excuse to be unhappy? It didn't make any sense.

I was playing OK for most of the final, but at 6–6 I slipped up a gear and it all fell into place. And John's head had gone. He was in front of his own crowd and they expected him to win because he'd just won the World Championship three months before. I guess he probably couldn't deal with it. It's like me playing at Wembley: you're desperate to win at home and it puts more pressure on you.

There was no reason on earth to be disappointed or miserable, but I was. And I had to put up this big front and pretend that I was happy. I always thought I had to be what everybody else wanted or expected me to be. After the final, at the Embassy banquet, people were saying, 'You've just won a tournament, you must be ecstatic now, Ronnie,' but inside it was hurting me. All I wanted to do was say, 'Thank you very much, I'm going to my room now,' but I didn't feel I could because I knew I was meant to celebrate, to party. I was thinking, I have to make a speech and say how fantastic the tournament is, and how great the sponsors are, and what a fantastic manager Ian Doyle has been to me, and what a rock he is, and thanks to the Scottish people, and I'm delighted to be playing in front of them, and I can't wait to come back here next year. But I couldn't wait to get out of the place, get back to my room and be miserable with Del. He could handle me; he knew what space I was in. He knew that I was putting up a front because he had lived with me during the whole week, and knew that winning the tournament wouldn't make it any better.

I got up to make my speech. John Higgins had just made his, and he had addressed the people so confidently as 'ladies, gentlemen and distinguished guests', and I thought, Fucking hell, what am I going to say? He said that it was a great tournament and he was delighted that I'd won it, and he made some funny jokes and everybody started laughing. He'd just been beaten and he was happy; I'd just won and I was a mess. I got up and said, 'Hello, ladies and gentlemen.' There were three hundred people sitting there, invited guests from the sponsor, Embassy, and I couldn't even look them in the eye. I think I said, 'Thank you very much' but I'm not even sure if I got that much out, and then I just added, '... Erm, and that's it.' I heard people laughing, and I was certain they were laughing at me. Looking back, I know they probably weren't laughing at me, but I was so paranoid.

Next morning Del was having breakfast but I wouldn't go downstairs because I felt so bad. I asked Del to send up my breakfast and told him that we'd head straight off. I'd won £65,000 in the first tournament of the season, I'd just had a three-month break and there could have been no better way to start the season, but I felt like death. After breakfast, Del said he'd just had a chat with the commentator and *Guardian* snooker correspondent Clive Everton. 'He listened to your speech,' said Del, 'heard what you said, and he said to me "I was in exactly the same position as Ronnie where I could not face people; I could not face anything. I'd be playing snooker and break down and cry for no apparent reason. He's depressed, and he needs to do something about it."' It sounded familiar: I'd had times like that when I'd be playing snooker and I'd just break down. That's when people thought I was a bit of a nutcase. I took on risky shots because I was thinking, Fuck this. I want to get out of here as quickly as possible.

Sometimes it would work to my advantage. When I got reckless, if the balls started flying in the opponent might think, This is an important match, he shouldn't be going for those shots, and he would be freaked. He'd miss balls because he was thinking I was fearless. But the only reason I was fearless on the table was because I was drowning in fear off it. I'd often get to 5–5 in an eleven frame match and would be happy knowing that I could pack my bags and go home and wouldn't have to stay around the tournament any longer. The money wasn't important: I knew if I lost every first-round match I'd still have enough to pay the bills. I was thinking, Well, the worst that can happen is I'll slip down the rankings, but I'll still make enough to get by.

When I got home I phoned Mike Brearley. (During their conversation that morning, Clive Everton had suggested to Del that I should get in touch with Mike, who since quitting cricket has worked as a psychotherapist, specialising in sports psychotherapy.) He said he was too busy but recommended me to a Dr Margo at a private hospital just round the corner from my home. I went to see him for about a month and poured my heart out to him. He just listened; barely said a word. He had a calming face, one you could trust, and I talked and talked. It cost a hell of a lot, but I hoped it was worth it. Every time I came out from seeing him I felt good. It was a weight off my shoulders. Then I'd go to bed, wake up, and next day the anxiety had started again, the panic attacks, the sense of isolation. It got to the point where I didn't want to do anything.

I eventually went to another psychotherapist, and to Mike Brearley himself. He came out with one thing I just couldn't cope with. I told him that I was struggling with my cue action and that I wasn't feeling good when I was around the table.

'Is your dad right-handed?' he said.

'Yeah,' I said.

'So there's a good chance he stabbed the man he killed with his right hand,' said Brearley.

'Yeah, probably.'

'Well, maybe what happened in the club that night is affecting your right arm. There were people in the war years ago who were made to shoot people and didn't want to do it, and years later their arms became paralysed.'

I couldn't get my head round that one, and after that I just couldn't take him seriously. It's not that he wasn't any good – I know he's got a good reputation and that he's helped out a lot of people – but as soon as he suggested that, I lost faith in him. I still went to see him for a year after that because my self-esteem was so low that I didn't have the bottle to tell him that there was no point in me coming to see him and that I didn't think we were making much progress. I even paid him more than his fee. I think it was eighty pounds a session, and I'd give him ninety because I wanted him to like me, wanted him to think I was a nice person.

'You don't need to give me extra,' he said.

'No, I feel better for doing that,' I said.

Again, that was due to my self-esteem. I thought the only way of proving I was a decent person was by paying him extra. If I gave things to people, they wouldn't think I was the arsehole that I thought I was.

Mike Brearley was all right. I generally felt better when I came out from seeing him, but I often drove up to see him in Islington thinking, Why am I driving all this way, in the rush hour, when I'm going to feel OK for a couple of hours or a day at best? Just like with Dr Margo, I didn't feel I was getting any long-term benefits from it, and I resented the fact that I had to go up there. Eventually, I admitted psychotherapy wasn't working for me.

Within a month of winning the Scottish Masters I went to Ireland to do some exhibitions. I took Del out with me. It doesn't matter if I'm miserable in front of Del – he takes away the pain. If you've ever seen the film *The Green Mile*, Del is like the black fella who sucks all the pain out of the others. We've been through so much. That is, he's been through so much with me. Without him, I know I wouldn't be playing the game today. Del's only addiction is to life; he just buzzes off people. He can see the funny side of everything, and I laugh so much when I'm with him. He's like medicine.

On the first night in Ireland, *bang!*, fantastic, I made a 147, got a standing ovation, everybody was going nuts. I made three more century breaks in the nine frames. I have to make centuries and maximums when I do exhibitions because I can't play trick shots and don't do gags. If I don't make centuries, the punters think, Well, when I watched Ronnie O'Sullivan he couldn't make a 50 and he didn't say a fucking word. Fantastic! So there's pressure on me to perform because otherwise what are they getting? With Dennis 'Lobster' Taylor, you might not see a 50 break all night, but you'll see some great tricks shots and he'll make you laugh. So that night my snooker was good and I was feeling good, on cloud nine.

Second night we went to Lilly Bordellos, drinking, smoking dope, with a handful of Irish friends tagging along, and they were all loving it. Del took off at around 3 a.m. but I was still going strong. From there we went to Leeson Street and stayed until seven in the morning. I was wide awake, flying, and I didn't want to go back to my room, so my mates said we could go to an early house. I had no idea what they were on about so they explained that these were pubs that opened at 7 a.m. 'Perfect,' I said: Guinness for an early breakfast. We were walking through the town centre first thing in the morning, as people were going to work. I was wearing a huge overcoat with nothing on underneath because my mate had thrown up on himself and I'd given him my shirt. We must have looked like four escaped lunatics. I thought, What must they think of us? But I was so far gone, I didn't really care. We sat in the pub drinking Guinness till noon. I was due to play another exhibition in the afternoon but of course when I got to the table I couldn't pot a ball.

And that was how we continued for five days and nights. On the last night I sat with my head in my hands. Del asked what was the matter. I don't think he realised quite how much I'd been caning it. I felt dead. I couldn't move. I said I couldn't go on, and that we should give the punters their money back. We went to the exhibition, got it out of the way, and

I flew home the next day. Back at home, I was on the settee and couldn't move, paralysed by what I'd done to myself for the whole week before. I had nine days before the start of the UK Championship. Nine days to get myself back together. It wasn't just the booze that was getting to me: I was depressed and physically exhausted, too.

I could scarcely get motivated to do any exercise because in my heart I knew it was all going to be for nothing. I was gone. I couldn't even practise. I wasn't emotionally up to another tournament, or anything else. And I knew that everyone would feel that I'd let them down. After all, I'd be entering the UK as the defending champion. I promised myself this would be the last time I'd let myself get into such a state. But before I even crossed that hurdle something worse had to be faced. Should I tell Dad how I'd regally fucked myself up? Should I wait for the day before the tournament and then tell him? Here I was, facing one of the biggest tournaments, and I was a total mental wreck. I thought, Where he is, the last thing he wants to know is that I've been out on a mega bender. But if I had to pull out of a tournament because of it, that would be the killer. I wasn't going to get any sympathy. I knew he'd just tell me what a mug I was, what a doughnut, that I was bringing shame on the family. I knew I'd get all of that, and I just prayed to God that he'd go easy on me.

Thinking back to it now, I wish I'd just kept my mouth shut, pulled out of the tournament and not told him why, because the reaction I got from him was even worse than I'd feared. I ended up blurting it all out: 'Dad, I was in Ireland last week and I tore the arse out of it, and I don't think I'm going to be able to play in the UK. I'm feeling shit mentally, I'm exhausted, and I can't even face picking up a cue. Dad, I mean it.' My depression was deepening, but I'd yet to realise that that's what it was.

'I do not believe this,' he said. 'I cannot believe that you go out and do this. I thought you had more sense.'

'Dad, I know,' I said, 'it was a mistake. I'm bang out of order, it won't happen again. Please God, don't let it happen again.' I told him I'd try to turn it around, but that was just talk.

He was on the phone every day after that asking how I was feeling.

'Yeah, I'm all right, I've been training a bit and resting,' I'd say.

But every day when he spoke to me something new seemed to have pissed him off. It wasn't just the week in Ireland, it was everything I'd done over the past six months that he'd decided had led up to this. Then one day he just let rip: 'You're a complete liability,' he said. 'Me and Mum don't think we want anything to do with you. You're in business with us, we're pulling our end together, but you're not pulling your weight. We can't take this any more. Mum wants you out of the house and we don't want anything to do with you. I don't want to see you on the visit any more. This will be the last time I speak to you.' He went on and on, getting more and more upset.

In spite of this, I told him I definitely wasn't playing in the UK.

'Right,' he said. 'Get your gear, go and live on your own. Wish you all the best and all the luck in the rest of your life, but you're not partners with us no more.'

Everything I had earned and everything Mum and Dad had earned we'd shared. We'd bought property together, and when I'd overspent Mum had helped me out with my tax bill. Everything went in the pot, and while Dad had been away I'd been the one buying the properties and investing the money.

'You're taking on all these mortgages and you can't even keep yourself straight for a fucking snooker tournament.' He was screaming at me down the phone.

I knew the inmates and the screws were listening to this, and the screws were probably getting off on it, thinking, He's cracking, he's finally cracking. Probably the only thing that could make Dad crack was something like this – the family falling apart.

I was devastated. I knew there was no way to sort it out. I resigned myself to the fact that I wouldn't see Dad again. I felt so pissed off with him and Mum. I'd always tried my best; and, yes, I'd been stupid, but I felt so low at the time, my self-esteem was down to zero, and my only answer to that was to get wrecked. I'd never spoken to them about why I was getting myself into such a state and how I felt about myself. They simply thought I, like many young lads, was into booze and a bit of recreational drug use, and that as long as I controlled it, it would be fine. But I was in such a bad place that the puff was becoming my medicine. It was becoming more important to me than snooker. I was so desperate for the instant, chemical high that I wasn't thinking of the consequences. I knew I was making it worse and worse and worse for myself, but I certainly wasn't doing it because I wanted to piss off Mum and Dad. They'd always say there were plenty of people worse off than me, and of course they were right, but it didn't make me feel any better knowing that I could afford anything I wanted. They couldn't understand that. It's very hard to understand how bad a depressive feels, and why a depressive feels so bad, unless you've been there yourself. In a way, the most unhelpful thing you can do is examine the depressive's situation logically, because depression has nothing to do with logic.

Mum certainly couldn't understand it. She said to me, 'Look what I've been through, and I've handled it all.'

I said, 'Yes, you've done brilliantly and I'm proud of you, but that's you, and Dad being away isn't the only problem. It's just that I feel in bits every time I get up in the morning. And every time I go to a snooker tournament I can't face people. That's not normal, thinking, Fuck the snooker. I just want to get smashed every day to take away the pain.'

Looking back now, Mum and Dad can appreciate

that I needed to go through all that to find the answer myself. If I'd listened to them, I would probably have packed in the game. They didn't want me to do that, but they thought that was what was making me miserable. Before the fallout, Dad had always said, 'Look, if the snooker is making you depressed, take over the business. Me and Mum have had a good run, we think you're ready.' I'm glad I never took that road. Things happen for a reason, and if I had done that maybe I would have given up everything and felt just as bad.

I moved away from home. Fortunately, I'd just bought a little cottage round the corner. I'd been lonely enough before I'd had the row with Dad, but now I felt a new level of despair. Mum had disowned me, Dad had disowned me. All I had was Del. So I phoned him. I told him I'd fallen out with the family, moved out of home, and that I was a wreck. At least he didn't give me the bollocking of my life, but he did want to know where I stood with him.

'Del, it's me and you,' I said, 'We go on a mission together.' But I felt so lonely.

Del phoned Ian Doyle, who was managing me at the time, and told him I wasn't going to play in the UK Championship and he had the job of telling the organisers that the defending champion wouldn't be turning up. The press had a field day, running large on the fact that I was exhausted and depressed, and the snooker journalists were writing pieces about my mental state. I opened the *Daily Mail* one day and there was a big double-page spread by a journalist who knew me well saying that deep down I was a nice person. That journalist, Tex Hennessy, had taken me out for dinner in Blackpool with his wife when I was 15. He wrote that in those days I had been a really confident young man, beating everyone in sight, but now, seven years on, I was a troubled soul. He wrote that he'd seen how I'd changed over the years, how I'd gone from high to low. As I was reading it I was thinking, Why has this happened to me? He concluded by saying that it all had to do with my dad, but I was fighting my demons and trying to pull through. Everything he wrote was bang on. I was watching other snooker players enjoying their life, buzzing when they were at tournaments. I could still remember that feeling myself, and I was jealous. I thought, You lucky bastards. I'm a different class to most of you, and here I am, miserable as hell.

That was something else that was doing my head in: everyone was saying that I wasn't fulfilling my potential, that I wasn't winning as much as I should. I was reading all these articles and asking myself questions. Why am I tormenting myself with snooker? Why am I still playing it? Why am I so unhappy? Why is this happening to me? Why can't I have Dad here enjoying the snooker? If he was out, I said to myself, I know I wouldn't be in this position. At times I felt my depression was nothing to do with him, but at others I knew so much of it was rooted in the fact that he was in prison.

I knew when Mum and Dad disowned me that I had

two options for the future. At that point I could have gone out and wasted myself, pissed my life up the wall, or I could make Dad eat humble pie. I was desperate to win the next tournament so he'd have to get on the phone, if only to Mum to pass on a message to say, 'Tell him well done.' I knew he'd do that because, whatever he'd said, he loved me.

After a few weeks Mum phoned me and asked what was wrong, why wasn't I talking to her, why wasn't I at home? She spoke to me normally, as if she'd forgotten all that had gone on.

'Dad's out of order,' I said. 'I don't ever want to talk to him again. As far as I'm concerned, I'm not part of the family.' After all, that's what Dad had told me. 'That's fair enough. I can deal with that. Just let me get on with my life.'

'Well, I don't want that,' said Mum, 'I want you to come home.' She started crying.

I'd gone on another fitness binge – out running every day, practising six hours a day. I was determined to prove Dad wrong. I didn't win the next tournament. In fact, I was beaten in the first round. But the fact that Mum took me back in was the really important thing.

CHAPTER EIGHT

In the Priory

It was 2000. I'd just met Bianca and thought a lot of her. She was staying at my place most of the time. I'd spent the last couple of years just about keeping my head together, but deep down I was still in bits, and what was worse was that I couldn't show her the state I was in. So every morning I'd get up before her and get my fix, if that's what you want to call a joint at nine in the morning. I needed it to function – or so I thought. I would never do it in front of her because I knew it wasn't right, wasn't normal. I had become dependent on this thing. My previous girlfriend had been as bad as me, but Bianca never touched it, and I knew she'd think less of me if she knew what I was doing. I felt that I'd started to live a secret life, and I've never been able to keep secrets.

I needed help. I thought maybe it was the depression that made me need a joint first thing in the morning, and then on through the day. So I phoned up the National Drugs Helpline and spoke to a girl called Sam who has since become a very good friend of mine. I explained to her that I thought the problem was centred on my snooker, because every time my snooker was good my mood was good, and every time my snooker was bad my mood was bad. I didn't know which came first. If I was in a bad mood I'd sit indoors and not speak to anybody, or go down the gym and train for two hours to try to pull myself out of it. Or I'd just go down to one of my friend's places and get hammered.

After listening to this over the phone, Sam invited me round to see her. I told her I thought I needed a joint to function or relax in people's company.

'I think you're addicted to drugs,' she said.

I was seeing three psychotherapists by this time and none of them had ever suggested this.

'Would you consider going into the Priory?' she said.

I'd heard of the Priory, and thought, No, that's not for me, that's for heroin addicts or crackheads. I only smoke joints. The Priory's not what I need. But there was something persuasive about Sam.

'You'd be in hospital for four weeks. Would you try it?' she said.

'Well, I'll try anything,' I said. 'I've tried hypnotists, psychotherapists, counsellors. Yeah, I'm up for anything.'

'Would you come to a meeting with me tonight?'

'Yeah, I'll come.'

'Right,' she said, 'we'll go to the meeting tonight and I'm booking you in the Priory tomorrow.'

'Hold on! I ain't going in the Priory tomorrow. That can wait, I've got things to do.'

'Come to the meeting,' said Sam, 'see what you

150

think, and if you're up for going to the Priory, you're going in tomorrow.'

I decided to go and tell my mum, but asked Sam if she'd come with me because I had no idea how Mum would react. To tell the truth, I was a bit scared. Round at Mum's we all sat down, I introduced Sam, told Mum she was a drugs counsellor, and said I might be going into the Priory. Mum just burst out laughing. It was a nervous laugh and I don't think she realised how desperate I was.

'Well, what do you think?' I said.

'Ron, if you want to go in there, you go in. I'll back you one hundred per cent, you know that,' she said.

But she thought it was all a bit of a joke – despite the fact that she'd kicked me out once and had said she couldn't bear to watch what I was doing to myself. But then it had been more my weight than the drugs that had offended her, and once I looked good and was in shape, as far as Mum was concerned I'd turned the corner. If I looked good on the outside, I must be good on the inside. I knew that wasn't the case. I still looked OK, but why did I need a joint in the morning before I could face the world, before I could relax in anybody's company? I felt panic attacks coming on me, and the only way to get rid of them was to have a joint. I could be driving along the road and for no reason I'd have to pull over. The panic would fill up in me and I wouldn't be able to breathe because I'd be hyperventilating. People would look in at me and I'd think, What are you looking at? I felt so paranoid and the dope definitely made that worse. It made me a lunatic. But when I wasn't stoned I was full of fear, alone, ill at ease with myself. I was so uncomfortable in my own skin. I just didn't like being me.

My first meeting was in Mile End, east London, on a Thursday night at 8 p.m. I didn't know what to expect. Sam said, 'Just come and listen, you don't need to talk. Have a cup of tea, and if you fancy talking, talk.' I sat next to her. People were hugging each other and asking how they were doing. They came up to me and I was scared. I knew I was in the public eye and thought they were looking at me differently, and thinking, What's he doing here? Then a woman at the front asked for some readings. People started explaining why they were addicts, what an addict was, then they read through something called the Twelve-Step Programme of Narcotics Anonymous. The woman then thanked everybody who'd spoken.

A man then shared his experience, strength and hope – that was the first time I'd heard that expression: 'John has come down to share his experience, strength and hope'. You're meant to identify with the speaker's experience. I just listened, and I didn't have a lot in common with this fella: he'd been abused as a kid, he'd been bullied, he was black and people had had a go at him because of it, he'd taken heroin and ended up in crack houses. I looked at him and thought, He's not like me, I've always worked, we're worlds apart. He finished his story and I thought, What am I doing sitting here? This ain't for me, it's for proper hardcore people.

We were in a massive circle. People introduced themselves, said they were an addict, and told their stories. Five or six people shared their stories and I still thought, Nah, I don't identify with what anybody has said here. I was even a bit bored, and just sat back, thinking, I'll listen to what they have to say, but I'm not going in that Priory, I know that for sure.

Then this fella said, 'My name is Terry, and I'm an addict. I remember days when the phone would ring and I'd be in bed and I'd just put the sheets over my head to block it out. I'd come downstairs, draw all the curtains, and wouldn't answer the door to anyone. And when that phone rang I was a wreck: I couldn't speak to anybody.'

As soon as he said it, I thought, I know that feeling. If he was like me, and look at how strong he is now, then surely there is hope for me. From being hopeless I became hopeful in the time it took him to tell his little story. I'd never got that sort of buzz from what anyone had said before. All the therapists had said it had something to do with Dad going away, but it didn't take a genius to realise that if somebody you loved was sent to prison for eighteen years, it was going to have some sort of mental effect on you. And it didn't take a genius to realise I hadn't coped with it very well. But the therapists weren't helping me to deal with it: they were just telling me stuff I knew about myself without showing me any way forward.

But once I listened to Terry and heard what he said, I was so hopeful.

The next person to share their story wasn't a crackhead or heroin addict, he was just into dope, so there was another identification. You *can* have a problem with dope, I thought. You don't have to be hardcore to be here.

I came out of that meeting and said to Sam, 'That was brilliant, I'm buzzing.' I'd not spoken once. I was too frightened to open my mouth in case people judged me, or thought I wasn't qualified to be there. I reckoned if I kept my mouth shut, I could go every now and again, and just listening to something like that would inspire me.

'Yep, I'm going into the Priory,' I said. 'But not tomorrow. I must go and tell Dad first. I'm not going into hospital without speaking to him because I know the papers will find out, and I want him to be OK with it first.'

We had a visit for the next day booked so I went down with my mate Michael. For an hour I wanted to tell Dad about it, but I just couldn't bring it up. I didn't know how to. Eventually, I said, 'Dad, I've got something to tell you.'

He said, 'Well, what's the matter? What's wrong?'

'I'm going into the Priory,' I said.

'Thank God for that,' he said. 'You're going to do the Twelve Steps? I've got mates in here who are on the heroin: they've been terrible and they go to their meetings and do the Twelve Steps, and, Ron, they're now the calmest people you could meet. They don't chase this and they don't chase that. They're happy. I'm made up for you. Go in there and get on with it. However long you're in there, I wish you the best of luck. Anything you do, I'm all right with it, but I know that's going to be good for you.'

Dad told me that every time I was on the telly, he'd sit and watch me with one of his mates who was on the Twelve Steps. 'He's not going to win today,' this mate would say, and Dad would ask, 'How d'you know?'

'It's his attitude, how he is, you can just tell he's out of tune, and he ain't going to win.'

And Dad told me he was always right.

'Fucking hell,' I said.

Dad told me this fella was coming out soon and suggested I let him take me to tournaments. 'Dad,' I said, 'you've made enough rickets in your life with some of your friends, and I've had enough of them. I don't want him round me, I don't want a bit of a lunatic round me. I'm quite happy as I am.' Even though I wasn't.

Turning down Dad's mate like that ended the visit on a bit of a sour note, but when I got home I still felt great. I was still buzzing from the night before. I felt calm and relaxed. There was no committee rattling in my head. There had been these voices in my head fighting with each other. I didn't know where to go, what to think. I couldn't think through the voices. They would freak me out. Now they had disappeared.

I phoned Sam and she said she'd arrange for me

to go into the Priory the next morning. There was only one more person I needed to tell – Bianca – so I went to her house in Walthamstow and explained what I was about to do.

She did her nut. 'You're no drug addict,' she screamed. 'You've got no problem.'

'Look, I'm going,' I said, 'and I want you to support me on this. I think a lot of you, and part of the reason I'm going in is because I've met you. You don't do drugs and I feel bad that I have to, and this will make me a better person. Maybe this is what I need.'

'Well, if you go in there, you and me are finished,' she said.

That's how we left it, and despite what she'd said I was on such a high when I got home I really felt like a joint. I knew I was going into the Priory tomorrow and it was going to be totally drug-free. I'll have to sleep there for a month, I thought, it will be like a prison, so what harm could a joint do me now? So I started skinning up, but just then Bianca came round and we talked it through. Finally she came round to the idea of me going in: 'If you think you need it, do it,' she said.

But the next day, I got up and was about to go when she said, 'Look, it's either me or the Priory.'

I sat there and thought about it. Within five minutes I picked up my bags and said, 'See you later.' I went back to Mum's and packed a suitcase full of gear. Sam picked me up and we drove to the Priory in Roehampton. She dropped me off outside the gates and I walked into the reception area. After I'd signed in they took me to my room, which was nice and comfy and had a telly. This is all right, I thought. Then they sent in two women doctors, who asked me to fill out a form about my problems. They read it and quickly said, 'Yes, you qualify for an addiction unit. The questions you've answered tell us that you have a problem with your drug of choice,' which, at the time, was puff. I drank, too, but I thought I was only going in there to get off the dope. I didn't see the drink as a problem. They said that I should stay in my room for the morning and in the afternoon maybe I should go to the Narcotics Anonymous meeting. 'Saturday is a half-day for us,' one of the doctors said. 'Most people will go to the meeting at two-thirty. If you feel like it, go over there. We suggest that you do.' I'd only ever been to the one meeting a couple of days before, so I thought, I'd give it a go.

The meeting room was full of people and it frightened me. A big lady with big lips, big glasses, big all over really, was talking. My gut was pounding and the butterflies were flapping around because I was thinking, I've got to open my mouth, I've got to say something. I listened to them sharing their experiences, talking about the states they'd been in and how much better they felt now. I braced myself, told people my name and said, 'I feel depressed, I have panic attacks, I feel that I want to have a joint now. I don't feel comfortable sitting in this room, but I want some of what you people have got. I can't believe that you lot were once like me. I'm here, I've got a month in the Priory' – these recovering addicts weren't in the Priory, they just used that room for their meetings – 'I feel scared, I don't know if I'm doing the right thing. I don't know whether I belong here. Whatever, I've given everything else a go and it hasn't worked. And I'm going to give this a go.' A tear started welling in my eye. Everybody was looking at me so intensely, and I was hoping to hell I hadn't put my foot in it, hadn't upset anybody with what I'd said.

But they all came up to me later and one person said, 'You give me so much strength.' I thought, What!? How can *I* give *you* strength? Are you taking the piss out of me? Then he said, 'You're in the right place, just take one day at a time.' The woman with the big lips and big glasses said, 'I've been clean for four years, but what you said took me back to what I felt when I first came into a room like this. And what you said is going to keep me clean today. I know that if I do what I did before I'll end up back where you are now. Seeing you in so much pain stops me wanting to go back there. That's why they always say that the newcomers are the most important people at the meetings, because when they tell their stories it's a reality check for the rest of us. This disease has got a bad memory and it will tell you that you're well when you're not, and it will tell you that you can go and do all these things when you can't. This is what I know today.'

After the meeting a fella came up to me and we

sat under a tree in the Priory's grounds. Everybody else had gone home. He sat there with me for about an hour and a half, and we just talked.

I said, 'I feel like shit. I think I'm going mad.'

'It's all right to feel like that,' he said.

'It's all right to feel fucking depressed and angry and fucked off and to hate the world?' I said.

He nodded.

Suddenly I understood. 'Yeah, it's OK to be pissed off, isn't it?' I said. It was like a revelation. As soon as I said it I didn't feel bad about being pissed off. I felt quite relaxed. I thought, If I can keep going to these meetings, keep hanging around with people like this and talking about this stuff, I'll be all right. And it wasn't like I was missing anything on the outside because my snooker was shit at the time.

'What about feeling that you want to take drugs?' I said.

'That's OK as well,' he said.

I thought, Fucking hell, everything's OK. Everything's going to be all right. I felt at home. I asked him how long he'd been clean.

'Fourteen months,' he said.

'Fourteen months, and you haven't had a thing?' I couldn't believe it.

'That's right. I come to meetings, speak to people like you, and I'm getting well. I have times when I'm still angry and pissed off, but it's OK to feel like that.'

I felt good for the first time in an age and thought, I'm going to give this my best. But then I always give

100 per cent to whatever I'm doing – that's probably why I'm an addict. I find it very hard to have one joint, or one drink, or one night out. I want to invite everybody around, I want to have the best party, the biggest party, I don't want anybody to go home. I do everything to the extreme.

I started to learn about myself at the Priory. Beforehand I didn't have a clue about how I functioned and what drove me. All I thought of was getting up in the morning, playing snooker, bringing in the money to pay the bills and making sure that Mum was OK till Dad comes home. That was my duty in life. I might have been feeling shit, but I felt I had to keep going, whatever. Until now.

Sometimes I beat myself up over my extremism, or perfectionism, call it what you will. Wanting to be the best, wanting to win, is an asset, but you can make yourself very unhappy when you don't reach the standards you set for yourself. Instead of making progress, you can set yourself back. Now, whenever I feel like that, I try to nip it in the bud so it doesn't spiral out of control.

At the Priory, the nurse would wake me up at 7.30 a.m. and give me my little tablet. They took me off the herbal remedy St John's wort that Del had recommended for my depression and put me on an antidepressant. (People call St John's wort a natural antidepressant, but it has never done anything for me.) There was one middle-aged nurse, and I'm sure she fancied me because she kept lifting the covers up when I was naked. She looked like a drag queen, and she made me feel quite uncomfortable. She kept catching me in the nude, and I started to wonder whether she was doing it deliberately. She'd come in when I was walking around naked and pretend she was shocked. 'Oh, Ronnie!' she'd say, but she wouldn't turn around, she'd just stand there talking to me. I'd have to run and get a towel and put it around myself. I'd be thinking, Get out, I've got a semi on here. Mind you, she soon got rid of that for me. Maybe that's what she was there for: coming off the drugs could turn you into a sex addict, so maybe she was there to cool off your desire.

You had to be up and ready for breakfast at 8 a.m. You didn't have to have breakfast, but they suggested that I should have a meal in me before I went to the therapy classes. We'd all meet at the Galsworthy Lodge. This was where the drug counselling and therapy sessions were held. If you were an alcoholic, you went to AA in the day; if you took cocaine or crack, you went to CCA – Crack Cocaine Anonymous – the hardcore meetings. I tried out all the groups, but ended up going to NA, Narcotics Anonymous, because that was the one I could identify with most closely.

There were about thirty of us there, and the sessions were all done collectively. There were too many people for one group so they'd have, say, one big group of sixteen and two of seven. I started off in one of the small groups. Everyone had a duty. Somebody would be the secretary and had to find out which meetings everyone wanted to go to.

Somebody else would be in charge of getting cigarettes, because we weren't even allowed out of the building for ten days. Even after ten days you had to go outside with someone who had been there for three weeks. You had to earn your trust gradually. It didn't bother me. I knew I was there for a month, and there was no point in running away. I thought, I'm going to dig myself into this and try to make it work for me.

We'd start at about 9 a.m. with our daily reflections. That was a little book of sayings and we'd read out a paragraph a day: for instance, 'Today we will hand our life over to the care of a higher power. Whatever we do today, we always know that our higher power will be with us through the good times and through the bad times.' Every day there was a different reading. They told us there was no cure for addiction and said the only thing that could help people with their addiction was to follow the Twelve-Step Programme. This is what I had trouble with: the philosophy. Because I believed what will be will be, I couldn't see the point of resisting your fate. That leads on to you thinking it's OK to have a joint, it's not going to kill you. Like most addicts, I was trying to bend things to my own needs – or at least my desires.

I think the Twelve-Step Programme is a kind of religious thing, but they would call it *spiritual* rather than *religious*. I told them I was an agnostic and there was no way that I'd get religious about this, and they said, 'You don't have to be religious. It's just about believing in a universal power or living the spiritual life. It's about being honest with yourself and the answers are within – it's at a gut level, a feeling level, and sometimes you might say yes to something that you may mean to say no to and in doing that you are not being honest with yourself. But there are other pressures to contend with: you might want to kick drugs but feel frightened without them or there might be peer pressure from supposed mates who want you to join in with them. Spirituality is about being honest with yourself, about asserting yourself.' All this – not being able to say no, feeling frightened, being pressured by mates to join in with them – sounded very familiar to me.

One of the Twelve Steps is to admit that you are powerless and that your life has become unmanageable. That is the first step you have to accept. Second, you have to accept that a power greater than yourself could restore you to sanity – so that's about opening up the mind to something greater than you. Something greater than me I would say would be an NA meeting. Three, you have to decide to turn your life and your will over to that higher power: so, I decided, I'm going to do what they say in these rooms because it's obviously working for the people here and they are getting well.

At one of the early therapy sessions there were three girls sitting at the back of the room. I was having a laugh with them and I fancied all three of them. At first, when I didn't have access to drugs, all I could think about was sex. I said something, thinking I was being funny, but they just stared at me. And I thought, Fuck, they've sussed me out, they must all know that I fancy them and they're going to stay away from me. As I was talking, I was sure they thought I was a pervert, but I couldn't understand why they thought it was wrong to look at a woman and think, Ooh, she's nice. They were all upper class and well spoken, and seemed to be something big in the publishing world. I thought, I'm not fitting in here. I became so paranoid and was convinced the girls would tell everybody else what I was really like, and that they would all agree with them. I'd only been there three days and knew I couldn't handle another twenty-eight, so I went to my room, my face was so red, and I was so hot, phoned a taxi, packed my bags and left.

When I got home, I said I'd never go back into the Priory. Sam, the drugs counsellor who had persuaded me to go there, came round to Mum's that night to try to persuade me to go back.

'There's no way in a million years that I'm going back in there,' I said.

'Why? What happened?'

I told her.

'That's you,' she said, 'you're paranoid. Just go back there and face them and you'll feel so much better.'

'No. I'll go to a different treatment centre. Find me another one. I'm not going back there.' I told her that I didn't have the bottle.

'You can go back,' she said. 'This is what recovery

is going to teach you. It's about taking risks and breaking through.'

Eventually she convinced me. Four hours later, at midnight, I was back there with my case, knocking on the door. Everybody wanted to know where I'd been, but I couldn't tell them. I felt ashamed. I couldn't even tell the doctors. When they asked, I just said, 'It's not important.' But it was important, and it was something I needed to talk about. So eventually I did confide in one of the doctors. 'I felt uncomfortable,' I told her. 'I said something and I believe they took it the wrong way and started making fun of me. I couldn't look at anybody after that, and there was no way I'd be able to go to therapy classes with that on my mind, so I just wanted to get out of here.'

'It's normal,' she said. 'It's normal for people to be like that in here. You're not in here because you're well. You're not a well person, and this is what we need to talk about while you're here.'

The next day the three girls were as good as gold with me. They just wanted to know where I'd been. I thought, I must be completely off the wall. I'd totally misread the situation. I didn't even mention why I'd run away. They obviously didn't know they'd caused the problem, so I just left it at that.

By returning to the Priory I felt I'd made a breakthrough. I didn't know what it was, but I knew it was one. The old me would never have returned to address the problem. I'd just have smoked a joint to forget how uncomfortable I was feeling. I was really raw at that time and everything that happened was magnified a thousand times. So for me to feel so humiliated and return without the anaesthetic of drugs was amazing. I was forced to confront how I was feeling and what I felt about these other people. When I told the nurse why I had run away, she understood completely. 'Your feelings are totally up in the air at the moment,' she said, 'and you just don't know what to do.'

I sat through more therapy classes, and broke down once when I talked about Dad being put away. They asked me what made me angry.

'I'm angry because of where my dad is,' I said. 'And I'm angry about how long they put him away for. I think it was a liberty. I've got resentment against the law and authority.' When I told them about what Dad had done at his trial I started crying.

Perhaps it's harder to survive on the outside than on the inside. I had to do a lot of adapting to survive without Dad being there, and I'd never foreseen that. I'd never thought I'd have to survive without him being there to crack the whip or to look after me, and at 15 years old that is a lot to take on board. Today I'd probably handle it very differently to how I did then.

We talked a lot about Dad in the therapy sessions. I think the therapists were trying to break me, to get right down to the nitty-gritty. It seemed to give them a buzz when I broke down and showed emotion because it made everybody else cry, too. To me, it was mad really, telling all these people I'd just met my most intimate thoughts and secrets. But breaking down in front of them seemed to bring us all a lot closer together. It reminded me of *Big Brother*, but without the booze. We were locked up together, forced to share each other's space, and you had to get to know everyone really well. But there was more kindness than in *Big Brother* – we wanted to help rather than shaft each other.

One day we were sitting on the grass having a cigarette. I said to a few friends I'd made, 'Come over to Ireland. You'd love Ireland. Come out there, watch some snooker, and have a few Guinnesses.'

'Don't you realise,' they replied, 'that it's total abstinence? You're not allowed to drink, you're not allowed to take drugs, you're not allowed to take anything that is mind altering.'

I'd been there a week by this stage and didn't have a clue. 'You're joking,' I said. 'I've only come here to stop the dope. I ain't come here to stop drinking. I ain't got a problem with that.'

'But one thing leads to another,' they said. 'Your drug of choice can change, or you could end up having a drink and then you'll have a smoke and then you're back on it.'

'That's complete bollocks,' I said. 'I've never liked drink anyway.'

That wasn't true: I used to drink like a fish. But I never thought it was a problem because it was never my first choice. I only drank if I couldn't have a puff. At the time, I couldn't get my head round the idea of total abstinence, but now I realise it's important.

I know from personal experience that having a drink leads to other things.

I became close to a lady called Rose. She was an alcoholic, 55 years old, and the first time I saw her in therapy it seemed as if all the others were picking on her. Sometimes she'd end up in tears. She would keep justifying why she needed to drink, but many of the people who'd been in therapy for years had heard every 'poor me' story there was going. She told us how, if circumstances were different, she wouldn't need to drink; said that we didn't know what her boyfriend was like, didn't know what a hard time he gave her; told us her son refused to talk to her. I felt sorry for her and stuck up for her, saying, 'No wonder she drinks: she's entitled to drink having to put up with all that.'

But the others said, 'She's going to kill herself; she's an alcoholic,' which I thought was going too far. She seemed tough enough to overcome anything.

'She's not going to kill herself,' I said. 'She's as fit as a fiddle.' I used to call her SuperGran because she was so fit. She played golf and after we came out of the treatment centre we had a few rounds together and built up a special relationship.

In the Priory Rose used to tell me I was like her son, and she used to do my laundry for me. I would get told off for this in therapy because it was something I should have been doing for myself, and it wasn't good for me to have someone do it for me. This was the sort of stuff we used to talk about in groups, and I thought it was funny because it was so different to the way I'd been brought up. Dad always had people doing stuff for him: he would charm them and they would think it was great doing this or that for him. But here they were telling me that it was wrong to allow Rose to do stuff for me and for me to sympathise with her situation. They told me I was enabling her to carry on pissing away her life, and that we had to break down her justification to drink. In recovery they say that if you enable people you allow them to deny their problem. I didn't see it like that. I just saw an old lady who needed a bit of love. But at the end of the day they were right and I was wrong.

Rose died last year. She drank herself to death. In the end her kidneys packed up; they couldn't take any more. I didn't go to her funeral. I still feel bad about it, but I can't cope with funerals. I should have gone, but I copped out.

Another great person I met in the Priory eventually became my sponsor for the Twelve-Step Programme. The sponsor is a role model who has made a good recovery and can guide you through the Twelve Steps. I chose a fella who had been in the Priory and came back every other Thursday for Aftercare – a support network for former inpatients. The first time I met him, I came into the room, sat in the big armchair and fell asleep. Even as I was doing it, I was thinking, This is so rude of me to be falling asleep. As I woke up, he said, 'It's all right if you want to go to sleep, it's no problem.'

'Who are you?' I said. 'Have you just come in here?'

'No, I've come in to do a share with you,' he said.

'Oh, all right then. Wake me up when you start, will you?'

'No,' he said, 'it's fine if you fall asleep.'

Everyone else came into the room. There were about six of us in this little tea room where we watched our telly and had a laugh. He started speaking and told us how he was, how he got into recovery and how his life is today. From being completely knackered and unable to keep my eyes open, I was engrossed in what he was saying because it was such a powerful message. They always told us to collect as many phone numbers as we could from recovering addicts to create a support network for ourselves, so when we left there would be people to ring for help when we were in a bad space. So I went up to him straight away and said, 'I want your number.' I knew when I left the Priory he would be the first person I'd ask to be my sponsor.

After the meeting we all went outside for a fag and met some of the other patients. I told them that I had heard the most unbelievable story in my life and that I was absolutely buzzing from it. 'I can't believe this fella used to be an addict,' I said. They were looking at me as if I were mad. But he seemed so calm and chilled out, and that was all I prayed for – just a bit of serenity in my life. I was always 100 m.p.h., always fidgety, always nervous. He had said that he could be in a massive traffic jam, knowing that he

Looking pensive in my room at Blackpool, where I was playing the qualifiers in 1992. I managed to win 74 out of 76 matches. Fuck, did I do well!; OVERLEAF practising at the same tournament.

LEFT My greatest fans, Jean and Ernie. Jean used to launder my shirts and always cried when I got beat (i.e. twice in 1976!).

MIDDLE Me with my nan, Angela and Granddad Vincence at a charity tournament in Birmingham. I went on to win the tournament.

BELOW Vince, a family friend. I'm holding April, Dad's goddaughter.

With Barry Hearn, at Leyton Orient's ground,
just after I signed with him.

On the plane with the Yunzi, my good friend, on the way to a
tournament in Thailand. The Yunzi helped me out when I was
going through a particularly bad time.

ROCKET

RONNIE

Cue ace pockets £515 a SECOND for fastest 147

▬▬ KEVIN FRANCIS

SNOOKER whizzkid Ronnie O'Sullivan roared into the record books yesterday with the fastest-ever 147 break.

He took just five minutes and 20 seconds to sink 15 reds, 15 blacks and all the colours. The astonishing feat earned him £147,000 for the maximum break and £18,000 for the highest TV break, making a total of £165,000.

That works out at an incredible £515 a SECOND.

Ronnie, 21, hit the jackpot during a 10-6 win over Mick Price in the Embassy World Championship at Sheffield's Crucible Theatre.

His shattered opponent gasped: "He isn't just on a different planet — he's in a

Turn to Page 3

Sheffield, a year later in 1997, and record-breaking again. This time, the fastest 147.

OPPOSITE PAGE TOP With Mum, after just having won the UK Championship in Preston, 1993. I was buzzing.

OPPOSITE PAGE BOTTOM Me and my mate Peter 'Psycho' Ebdon, 1996.

Me with Prince Naseem at the Crucible in Sheffield, in 1998.

With my best mate George.

In the garden of the Priory, with my mate Paul.

was late for an appointment, but he also knew that he couldn't get there any faster, so he'd just hold his hands up and surrender: acknowledge that he couldn't get there on time but would get there when he could. 'The whole world's not revolving around me,' he said, 'and by jumping the traffic lights I'm only going to get nicked or cause an accident to try to get there fifteen minutes earlier, and if I get there fifteen minutes late I can explain to the fella why I was late.'

It was such a simple story, but it was me down to a T. Whenever I was in a car I was like a raving lunatic. I wanted to be everywhere in five minutes. I was road-rage material. So I thought, Right, that's what I have to do in that situation – surrender. And it didn't just apply to traffic jams; it applied to life in general. It can just as easily apply to snooker as to traffic jams. I can practise until I've got blisters on my hands, but then I just have to say, Enough's enough, this isn't good for me. I've got to put down my cue, get a bit of sanity into my brain, and come back fresher. But the addict in me wants to keep on playing and playing until I destroy myself. That's just how I am: I can destroy myself mentally over anything.

When I first went into the Priory hardly anybody knew who I was. They had all spent the past few years out of their boxes, and didn't watch telly or pay much attention to newspapers. It was weird for me because I'd always got by on people recognising who I was. I'd get chatting that way, rather than starting from scratch and being myself. But at the Priory nobody had any expectations of me: they just took me how they found me, and I got on well with virtually everybody there.

There were, though, a couple of people who didn't like me, who thought I was a flash Essex boy. One of them said to me, 'You're the big "I am", aren't you? You've got this and you've got that, and you think you're someone to be reckoned with.'

'No, I don't think that,' I said. 'That's what you think.'

He just looked at me and couldn't say anything. One of the therapists gave me a look as if to say, You've done him, and just started laughing. I didn't mean to do him. It was the only answer I could give because it was true: that was what he thought about me, and the last thing I thought about myself.

We ended up getting on all right later, perhaps because he'd had the guts to tell me what he thought of me, rather than being nice to my face and then bitching about me behind my back. I knew he'd been bottling something up, but at least when he let it out I knew where I stood with him. He turned out to be quite a nice fella in the end.

Sometimes the days went really slow, sometimes they went fast. Some days I would go back to my room at four-thirty in the afternoon, lie on my bed, and think, This has knocked me for six. But then Dad would ring up after a session, and we'd talk for ages. We were having good chats for the first time in years.

A session would last from nine-thirty to twelve-thirty. Then we'd all sit down for lunch for an hour and have a fag in the garden. We'd take it in turns to pick the dirty plates up from the table, wash the dishes and dry them. Then there'd be another therapy session until four-thirty. Six hours of therapy a day. Some classes would be heavy, some light.

One afternoon we played rounders, but even that was a test because they were examining our behaviour. One of the top people said she had never seen anyone like me in her life. 'Gazza was here, and not even he was as competitive as you,' she said. She was fifteen years clean, having been an alcoholic, and we got on famously. She wasn't one of our main therapists, but basically runs the Priory now. Everyone was shit scared of her, but you knew where you stood with her. She took no nonsense from most people, but I half got away with it. I don't know why, but she took a liking to me. The first time I saw her I thought she was a patient. 'Who's that?' I said. 'Cor! She's nice, isn't she!' She wasn't beautiful, but she had lovely legs and a tiny skirt on, and I thought I'd love to have a bit of that. Bold as brass I went up to her and said, 'You've got lovely legs.' She didn't respond and the others in the group whispered to me that she was the top therapist. Oh shit, I thought, I hope I've not put my foot in it. But obviously there was nothing I could do at that point, so I just hoped that she liked to be told she was fanciable. I mean I was in this nuthouse, and I was steaming after a while.

There were times I felt awful, and I just wanted to run away – especially after Bianca came to visit me, and I had to say goodbye to her, and I knew I wouldn't see her for another week. In the end, she had agreed to me going in, but I thought, Maybe I'm being a bit selfish in here, and it's time for me to get out.

Three weeks into the treatment I thought again, This isn't doing anything for me. It was such a struggle staying there. If I still felt like this after three of the four weeks, how could it work for me? It was so intense there. We were allowed to play games like Monopoly, but nobody ever felt like it. There was a gym, but they said we could only go in during our lunch hour and mustn't do more than half an hour because working out can become an addiction like anything else. So I was missing lunch and going in the gym to get out some aggression.

One day I said to the head therapist, 'I still feel like shit.'

'Come and have a chat with me,' she said. 'What's wrong?'

'Well, I feel that my snooker determines how I am as a person. If my snooker is good, I'm in a good mood. If my snooker is bad, I'm in a bad mood.'

She said it was a normal pattern for people, especially sportsmen, to associate their mood with their job. 'What you've got to do is detach yourself from snooker. You are Ronnie. Get to know Ronnie as a person. Ronnie the snooker player is different from

Ronnie the person. And even if you didn't play snooker you would still be Ronnie the person.'

'You're right,' I said.

It made sense. What really helped was that she told me what I was doing with my life and myself. I already knew it, but I couldn't put it into words. I didn't want to play snooker because I felt scared that as soon as I left the Priory I would fall back into the pattern of thinking of myself solely as Ronnie the snooker player, and that my only value lies in my snooker, so if my snooker's no good, I'm no good as a person.

Some days I felt in control of myself, others I didn't. One day I would get what all the treatment was about, the next I wouldn't. The therapist would come down and look at me some days as if to say, You're in a lot of pain. And she was right. I couldn't even talk to her, couldn't even look her in the eye. Then other days she'd come down and say, 'You've got it!' and I'd say, 'Yeah! How d'you know?' She could just tell by the way I looked. And once I thought she understood me, I felt I was in the right place.

At the end of the daily meetings, we'd all meet up in a huge room and sit down in a circle, and the head of the group (we used to vote who would be head of the group each week) would go over what we had done that day, then everybody would have to say their name and talk about how the day had been for them. It came round to me, and I'd say, 'My name's Ronnie and I've had a right poxy day today,' or 'My

name's Ronnie and I've had a fantastic day today.'
Towards the end of my stay I found more often than
not I was saying that I'd had a fantastic day.

CHAPTER NINE

Getting My Life Back

After a month in the Priory, I came out feeling like a human being again. I loved myself. I went to visit Dad and felt so good standing there, handing in my visiting order, being polite. It was just me being me, whereas before any little comment anyone said to me I'd pick up on and think they were having a dig.

After the progress I'd made in the Priory, I'd decided it was more important for me to be happy as a person than for me to be a snooker player. When I saw Dad on my first visit after coming out I said to him, 'I don't think I want to play snooker any more. You understand me, don't you?'

He just looked at me. 'No, I don't,' he said.

'What d'you mean, you don't understand me? Dad, if I want to do that, and that will make me happy, isn't that the most important thing?'

'Yeah,' he said, 'but I can't see why being happy has to stop you from playing snooker.'

I thought he was mad. I had all this happiness, was beginning to feel complete as a person, and the last thing I wanted was to go back to how I had been. But I listened to him.

Throughout my month in the Priory, I'd not

touched a cue. I refused to go near a table when I was there. I never played in the summer anyway. I always had two or three months off. When I came out I started practising again, and I was playing crap, but I was still happy. I thought, This is progress. In the past I would have been beating myself up massively.

Then the tournaments started and I played out of my skin. The first tournament after I came out was the Champions Cup. I made it through to the final and I've never felt as emotional as I did during that match. But I did get off to a disastrous start. I was 4–1 down to Mark Williams, and I looked up and saw three of my closest friends from the Priory sitting up in the stands – Charles, Martin and Rose. Until then I didn't have a clue that they were there. God, I thought, they think I'm one of the best snooker players ever and I'm getting stuffed here. Looking up spurred me on: I won the next frame. Martin and I used to call each other 'slag' in the Priory, so as I was looking up I mouthed, 'You Slaaaagggggg!' to him and he started laughing. He mouthed the same back. After every frame we had this exchange. I was pumped, my adrenalin was flying, I was on such a high, and I thought, I'm enjoying this. Mark Williams wasn't – he'd been playing brilliantly, the best I'd ever seen him play – and I started coming back at him, and ended up winning 7–5. I won six out of the last seven frames. Everything seemed to be working perfectly – my safety, my long potting, my break-building.

After the match, we all celebrated with a cup of tea. This was the new me. We spent about forty-five minutes together and then Charles, Martin and Rose went back to their treatment centre.

When I came out of the Priory, all the snooker pros knew where I'd been because it had been in the newspapers. I spoke to Jimmy about it, of course, and he was the first to make sure I was all right. He asked me lots of questions and was very supportive. Not many of the others said anything, even though I'm sure a few of them understood what I was going through. Playing snooker for a living is such a strange profession, and we've all got some tick or other. There's so much free time then suddenly you're playing at an incredibly tense level during the season. Sometimes you're sitting there, and you're feeling bad, and you need something to do. Stephen Lee has definitely got a thing about his grub. Willie Thorne is a lovely fella, but he loves a flutter. It's his thing. I've been on tours with him when he's been on the phone 24/7 just writing down bets. Perhaps you need an addictive personality to play snooker at a high level – it's such a difficult game that you need to have been addicted to it to have put in the hours to reach a competitive standard.

Addicts don't come away from treatment cured. They are always addicts, even if they've not given in to their addiction for decades. They say addiction is an illness, and you don't get any holidays from it. After the Priory I had seven or eight months' total abstinence and I felt great. It gave me back my life.

But inevitably I lapsed, and felt terrible when I did. I spoke to fellow recovering addicts, and they said, 'Look, don't worry, it happens, you can start all over again. Pick up the phone if you feel you want to do it,' but the last thing I'm going to do is pick up the phone to somebody who's going to try to talk me out of doing it.

It's vital for me that this doesn't become a pattern. I know I've got my life in control now, but when I go out in certain circles with certain people, I have to be honest and say that the temptation is there just to think, Oh bollocks, forget recovery, I can always go back to that, I can go back to the meetings or the Priory and get professional help and start all over again. When I'm left to do things for myself I think I can hang around my old friends who I used to do drugs with and I'll be OK. I convince myself, Yeah, I can handle them, and be around them while they're doing it, and I don't have to do it. But even when I'm saying it I know it's rubbish; I know I'm deluding myself. I've slipped on a few occasions since I left the Priory, but every time I've gone back to the drawing board and started all over again. And I've felt a hell of a lot of guilt.

An addict's life is a constant battle – a battle to stick to the Twelve-Step Programme, a battle to do what's best for yourself, a battle to keep well. My life was battered and I was unhappy, and was told by the professionals at the Priory that if I followed this programme I'd recover my equilibrium. But however hard I've tried, I know there have been times when I've turned my back on it. Because the programme is a spiritual thing, you're meant to open your mind up to this huge power and hand your life over to it, which I find difficult. And every time I've had a relapse, or a slip, or whatever you want to call it, I've been filled with guilt.

If I slip, the greatest guilt I feel is always towards my girlfriend Jo. We met through Narcotics Anonymous. It's a big part of why we're together, because we've both been down that slippery slope. She's brilliant, and hasn't had any relapses in two years, which, in a way, makes it even more difficult for me. If I do have a little slip, I want to talk to her about it, but I worry that she'll be so disappointed with me. And if I don't tell her exactly what I've done, and it's in my head and I don't let it all out, I become agitated, quite fiery and hard to live with.

Part of me is always hankering after something more. I'll be thinking, I'm only 27, I'm too young to miss out on all the things I see my peers going out and doing. But really I'm not missing out on anything because if I look at it sensibly, and look at where that life took me, it led me to complete misery. I would try to convince myself that I'd just have one night out, just one mini-binge, and this time it would be different; I'd get back to the recovery programme and treat it with more respect than I ever had done.

The programme should offer you so much, and although I'm in a much better state now than I was a couple of years ago, I know I'm not reaping the full benefits. I'm no longer in touch with the people from the Priory. I didn't use the Aftercare, which I probably should have done, but it was so much of a drive to Roehampton, and I'd be knackered after a game of snooker. But I have kept up with my local meetings. I use the Priory at Southgate now because it's closer to me, and I get the same back-up as I would do in Roehampton.

I still don't know enough about it to say what is right and what is wrong. I just know what I have to work on. For example, there is a mate who keeps ringing me up for a game of golf. Now, I know that the chances are if I play golf with him I might end up lapsing, and I know the excitement of talking about drugs, or talking about getting this bird or that bird, and doing all the wrong things, will lead to someone having a puff. I will feel uncomfortable turning it down, and I will end up having that joint. That is still my weakness. I work it out beforehand, know it will reach that situation, and say to myself when it comes to that point I'll say I've got to go, but once I'm there, and I'm involved in that situation, what worries me is that I'm likely to think, I ain't going nowhere.

Hopefully, by the time you're reading this, I will be a fully recovering addict, but at the moment it is still only partial. Part of being an addict involves knowing that a tiny part of the urge can always resurface unwelcomed. I can't even have a glass of wine because if I do I want more. I'm determined that this week I won't screw up – I'll go to my meetings and do my Twelve Steps. It's like home-work. I have to write all these things about denial, about reservations, about powerlessness, and every time I write it down, I think, I can't go and do that, I'm setting myself up. Once it's written down on paper and it goes into my brain, whenever my mate does ring for golf, because I've put the groundwork in, because I've done the homework, I've now got my boundaries and I know where that is going to take me. And I have a choice today – whether I want to play golf with him and indulge or play golf with someone who I know isn't going to offer me a joint. Then again, I could just go to my meeting. I don't want to put my hand back in the fire. All right, it might only be one joint, but I know one joint could lead me to a binge.

This mate knows that Jo and I met through Nar-cotics Anonymous, and he knows Jo doesn't do drugs any more. He makes me feel uncomfortable. I haven't got the bottle to tell him that I'm an addict because I feel half-ashamed, and I'm convinced that he's going to think I'm a complete mug. But Jo keeps telling me I must confront it and tell people, so I'm being honest with myself and putting the pressure on them – if they offer it to me then, it's them rather than me who will feel shitty.

I should go to the meetings every night, but I don't. I will go tonight, though. There is a counsellor I see at the Priory, and this week I told him I was feeling weak. He said, 'If you use anything before Monday, promise me you will come into the Priory for a week.'

I said there was no way I could promise him that because of how vulnerable I was feeling. But this weekend I'm going to prove to myself that I can go to my meetings and keep well. I'll feel great if I manage that. And I know if I give in I'll feel absolutely shit. The last time I gave in I was out all night. Jo got the hump because she didn't know where I was. It would be all right if I could go out and have a joint and a few beers and at 2 a.m. say, 'Right, I'm coming home.' But that's not really me. I wish it was. I wish I had that sort of balance.

Drug addiction makes you deceptive as a person, and I hate that because I'm compulsively honest by nature. That is the way I was brought up.

I've now been to well over five hundred NA meetings and I've heard all the terrible stories there are to hear. I've seen friends die. Somebody I was in treatment with died after he left the Priory. The first time I saw him in a meeting I thought it was a set-up – he was a millionaire, 30 years old, a good-looking fella. He had so much money that the Priory was like a hotel for him: he'd stay for a while, go home, then come back in again. I thought he was having a laugh. Then six weeks later he died from kidney failure: 30 years old, an alcoholic.

It hit me badly. This really is a matter of life or death, I thought. This fella's death made me aware of how easy it would be to return to my old self: start bingeing again, put loads of weight on, drinking, taking drugs, start hating myself again. That kind of life *is* death for me. I felt like death when I was in that condition, and I *wanted* to die when I was like that.

The weekend is over. My golf friend rang and left three messages, and I deliberately didn't get back to him. I've managed to get through without lapsing, and I'm feeling bloody good about it.

CHAPTER TEN

Players

JIMMY WHITE

The first player I met who really blew me away was Jimmy White. I was at a tournament in Birmingham playing in the under-16s event. All the top professionals were there, all the top juniors, all the top ladies. It was snooker's equivalent of Wimbledon.

I was practising and Jimmy came in the room. He had a pair of jeans on, an old shirt and an old pair of cowboy boots, a short leather cue case and an entourage of about five. He looked really rough, but good with it: designer rough. He came over, and he said, 'Hello, my name's Jimmy White. I've heard a lot about you, Ronnie.'

I was 14 at the time, and I was speechless. Steve Davis was my favourite player, but Jimmy was my idol. He was the first great player who came up and spoke to me like a human being. He was interested in me, interested in making friends. I asked him if he wanted my table to practise on, and he said, 'Lovely, nice one.' I stood and watched him practise and he didn't miss a ball for five frames. He was unbelievable. At the time he was winning everything – well, everything except for the World Championship, of course.

The next time we met was in Blackpool in the European Open, when I was 16. I'd only lost one in about fifty matches, and this was Jimmy's first match of the season. I beat him 5–1, and the match only lasted about fifty minutes. I was as confident as I could be, but I still never dreamed I'd beat him. I hadn't thought how hard it must be for him coming to play in a box room. I wasn't used to big arenas, so for me it was like my Crucible Theatre, but for him it must have been like: 'I've got to play this little 16-year-old, he's won all these matches on the bounce, everybody's talking about him,' and the pressure must have really been on him. I was flying after the match. Jimmy said, 'Well played,' to me, but nothing more.

Then, when I turned professional a short while later, he did interviews in which he said, 'Ronnie O'Sullivan is a breath of fresh air for snooker, he's fantastic for the game,' and as soon as I broke on to the professional circuit we became quite friendly.

I was still in awe. I still didn't feel comfortable around him or any of the other top players. They all talked to each other, and if I got a little hello in I was made up.

At Preston in 1992 I was playing in the UK Championship and had to play Cliff Wilson to get on the telly and into the last 16 against Stephen Hendry. I sat at breakfast in the Posthouse Hotel, just opposite the Guild Hall venue, and on the next table there was a fella called Harry the Dog. Now, Harry the Dog was a gambler, a big, fat, soft, cuddly bear of a gambler. But he was serious. I heard him say, 'Right, I want fifty grand on this one, this one, that one and that one, and Ronnie O'Sullivan.' It was an acker – where you put a bet on ten names that you think you can't lose on. He thought it was money in the bank for him – a simple way of turning fifty grand into a hundred and fifty grand. And I was thinking, Fucking hell, has he just had fifty grand on me? That's a bit heavy. I didn't know Harry the Dog at the time, but later I was told that's his job: he goes round every tournament betting on players.

After the first session I was 4–4 with Cliff Wilson. I had been 4–1 up. I also had a 145, which was the highest break of the tournament so far, and I was playing really well, but then he just started potting balls from everywhere. We came back the next evening to finish off. We were all gathered round the practice table waiting to be called out for the evening session, and Jimmy White was standing there. He looked at me and said, 'Is there any fucking chance of you beating this fat, bald, half-blind geezer?'

I said, 'What?'

Then it dawned on me. The day before I'd seen Jimmy on the practice table and he had asked some-body to put a four-grand bet on for him. I twigged that his bet was riding on my match. And I shit myself. It did my head in.

Jimmy was playing David Roe on the other side

of the arena. You could walk around the hall to watch all the matches, and after every frame of his match he came around to my table to see if I was doing the business for him. My match went 5–4, 5–5, 6–5, 6–6, 7–6, 7–7, and while this was going on Jimmy was playing his match. I realised that all the gamblers had put me in as a banker for this match.

I ended up losing 9–8. I was gutted. Jimmy ended up winning 9–8 against David Roe, and then went on to beat John Parrott in the final. So it wasn't too bad for him in the end, but he made me feel terrible during my match. Especially as I was walking out. He put so much pressure on me. If I'd had a bet on a player, I wouldn't even tell him. Thanks, Jim!

Everybody started laughing after the match. Players like Willie Thorne found it funny, but I found it intimidating. I never told Jimmy how bad it made me feel. It didn't alter my opinion of him really – he was still a hero, and I still wanted to be his mate because I liked him. I'd never forgotten the way he came up to me and spoke to me when I was 14.

People often ask why Jimmy never won the World Championship. He got to six finals and lost every one. I think part of the reason was that he never took the rest of the season seriously enough. By the time he got to Sheffield he had rarely competed in enough matches or won enough tournaments.

When I started playing at Sheffield I would see Jimmy playing in a local club, best of nines and best of elevens for £500 or £1,000, and I used to think,

Fair play to him. Then I realised he was just trying to get in as much match practice as he could for Sheffield. It was as if no other tournament mattered. A month before Sheffield he'd start practising and you'd think it was a different Jimmy, and if he had had that attitude at the start of the season and that discipline, I'm sure he would have won the World Championship, and on more than one occasion.

He put so much emphasis on winning the World Championship that it became an obsession. It was something he wanted so badly that in the end it did his brain in. A couple of times he panicked in the finals. At one point he was 14–8 up against Stephen Hendry. I know Hendry then played well, but Jimmy should never have lost from that position. I don't care how badly Jimmy was playing, he was still capable of winning another four frames.

He had more ability than any other snooker player I've seen. Technically, Stephen Hendry, Steve Davis and John Higgins were far superior. They know their game inside out, whereas Jimmy just played off ability rather than strategy. But of all the players I find Jimmy the hardest to play because when he plays well there is not a safe ball on the table. He's not just a good potter, though. He has the safety game, and the break-building, and he can win tournaments, but I think he has lacked that bit of discipline as a player. It's unfortunate he's never had someone like Del, my coach and mate, in his life.

All top players have hangers-on. The more popular you are, the more you have. Jimmy had more hangers-on than anybody I've seen. A lot of them are nice people, but I remember going up to Sheffield to watch him play John Parrott in the final of the World, and there were five or six fellas sitting in Jimmy's player's box, all starting on the beer, and saying, 'Jimmy's got this one in the bag and we're going to be celebrating.' Within an hour Jimmy was 7–0 down. He needed someone around him who could make him refocus. There's plenty of time to party after the World Championship when you've got three or four months to do what you like.

The final is a weekend of intense snooker, and you don't even want your families and friends down there. Mine only came down on the last day and I told them I didn't even want them there then really. I'm gutted for Jimmy that he hasn't won the World because he's a friend of mine, and I know how much it means to him. And to his Dad, Tommy.

Until I won the World Championship I said to myself, 'Well, is it that important to win the title? I don't think so. Your health is more important, there are all these terrible things going on, and you're worried about the World title.' I was trying to kid myself, but it never worked. And having won the World I know exactly what it means. At the end of a snooker player's career, the first question people ask in assessing his achievement is 'Did he win the World?'

I was in a similar position to Jimmy in my final against John Higgins. I was 14–7 up and nearly threw it away. It's a different kind of pressure, but eventually I came through it. And hopefully, having won it once, I'll handle the pressure better next time I get to a final.

It's sad for Jimmy because I don't think he'll ever win the World title now. The years have gone by and the older you get the tougher it becomes to keep up your mental strength. And there are just too many quality players. If there were only two or three around who were really good, like in the days when the Nugget was king, then, yes, of course he could do it. But I don't think you'll ever get a Dennis Taylor winning the World these days because that was when Steve Davis was head and shoulders above everybody else and if you beat him, you invariably won the World title. But today, if you beat Stephen Hendry, you've then got Mark Williams, Peter Ebdon and John Higgins. Having said all that, I'd love Jimmy to prove me wrong.

Jimmy is a snooker genius, but he fell just that little bit short so many times. And, in the end, I don't think he can blame anyone but himself. If you're better than your opponent, you should win. Look at Tiger Woods – he's so much better than everybody else and he's won so many Grand Slams because he makes that ability count. When it comes down to the last nine holes in golf, they say that's when the tournament begins, and I believe that's the same with snooker. Get to the quarters and semis of the World and that's when Stephen Hendry is doubly dangerous because he can scent victory.

*

Once, I was up in Aberdeen for a tournament. My match against Paul Hunter was due to start and Del came up to my room to wake me up. He'd been downstairs, mingling with all the players. Del can talk to anyone. I've seen him have lengthy conversations with people who don't even speak English, and he's come away and said, 'Oh, I had a really nice chat,' and I've said, 'Del, she doesn't even speak English and you don't speak her language,' and he's said it hadn't made any difference! If I said to Del at 3 a.m., 'We've got to go and hit some balls,' he'd be straight out of bed and there for me. That's why I love Del to bits. Dad once said if you told Del to stick a cucumber up his arse and walk round the arena because it made you play well, he would do it for you. 'I know he would,' I said to Dad. 'What more could you ask for?' Dad said. 'You've got a good man there in your corner for you.'

Anyway, Del was banging on the door and there was no answer. At 7.45 p.m. he let himself in the room and I was in bed. He said, 'Ron, you're playing in fifteen minutes, come on get out of bed.'

'I'm not playing,' I said, 'I'm *not* playing.'

'You've got to play,' he said. 'You're on the TV table. They're all waiting for you down there and asking where you are.'

'Tell them I'm not playing,' I said. 'I'm not in the mood.'

I was scared of going out and making an idiot of myself. Mentally, I just wasn't up for it. I'd been playing professionally for eight years and the game wasn't making me happy. Del was tickling my feet at the end of the bed, and telling me I had to get up. Eventually I put my gear on, buttoning my waistcoat up in the lift with Del doing my bow tie for me. I hadn't even had a chance to hit a practice ball because it was so late.

I was beaten 5–3, having been 3–0 down. The maddest thing was that at 3–0 down I started to feel good and fancied winning the match; something had clicked into place. But the damage had been done. If it had clicked that little bit earlier there was a good chance that I could have gone on and won the tournament, but I just self-destructed. I told myself it was bad luck, but of course it wasn't – it was my own fault because I'd set myself up to lose. I came off the table half positive but also pissed off. I'd really done myself up like a kipper. I had it in my mind that I was going to play badly, so I never gave myself a chance. I went to Jimmy's room and told him how pissed off I was: 'I'm lying in bed thinking, I don't want to be here.'

'Ron, I'm exactly the same,' he said. He'd just lost that night, too.

'But you say you love the game,' I said to him.

'There are times when I love it, but there are times when I hate it. It's a bastard of a game, but when I'm playing well I love it.'

'I was like that tonight,' I said. 'I didn't want to go and play, Del had to drag me out of my bed. I feel I'm playing useless and all of a sudden I start to click but it's too late.'

Jimmy and I chatted for a couple of hours until finally I said, 'Jimmy, I don't think I can do it no more.'

'Look, I know what you're saying. I've got another six or seven years in the game and just want to do as well as I can. But you've got a lifetime ahead of you. Just enjoy it as much as you possibly can.'

'But all I want to do is go out and enjoy myself,' I said, 'and I can't even manage that.'

Snooker was getting in the way of life. It wasn't as if I could get out of my box after being beaten in the first round in Aberdeen because I had a tournament the week after. The way I saw it, it was nine months of torture for three months of pleasure when I could do what I liked. It wasn't a healthy attitude.

You wouldn't have called me a professional. I was basically just someone with ability who could turn it on now and again. That was the only way I kept my ranking in the top five. But just sitting there with Jimmy, offloading, took the power out of what was bothering me. I went back to my room, kipped, got up the next day and cracked on.

The first time I reached the semi-finals of the World Championship in 1996, I got a phone call in my room. 'There's a Mr White on the phone for you,' the switchboard said.

Jimmy came on. 'You've been playing fantastic,' he said, 'just go and win the World. It's a bit different out there with just the one table, but you're playing fantastic stuff and we're all rooting for you back here. If you get to the final, I'm on my way down.'

I thought that was such a nice thing for him to say. He'd been beaten early on and had gone home. It gave me such a buzz and I walked out with a spring in my step. But I still lost.

I try to do the same to people I get on with in the game. That's something that Jimmy has passed on to me – to be a sportsman. If someone does well who I think deserves to do well, like John Higgins, I'll ring him up and say, 'Blinding! I'm well happy for you.'

After Jimmy was beaten at the start of the World Championship in 2001 he said, 'All I want now is for Ronnie to go on and win it.' He said he was going on holiday and he'd only be watching if I was playing. 'If he gets to the final I'll be cutting my holiday short to come back down to support him,' he said.

And who should pop in just before the evening session of the final starts? Jimmy came into the dressing room, wished me the best of luck and said, 'We're all supporting you. You've done fantastic already but go and win it now.' Just thinking about it makes me quite emotional. He came down with Ronnie Wood, who'd croaked, 'Yeah, just go and do the business, Ron.' I thought back to the time Jimmy and I had played the best snooker of our lives when we were smashed out of our heads at Ronnie's place.

After I won the World, obviously I thought of Mum and Dad, but I also thought of Jimmy, because I knew how much he had wanted to win the title. Every snooker player says if it's not to be their year to become World Champion, they'd like to see Jimmy do it. Everybody loves him. He gets on with every-one, and he's one of the funniest people I know. He's like an older version of me. He may be 40, but he's still ducking and diving all the time: having a game of cards in his room with thirty people crammed inside, and trays of room service outside. You know Jimmy's room because you just see tray after tray of food piled up outside. He just enjoys himself and likes to have fun.

Even though he hasn't won the World, he's not bitter. Take any player – from Dennis Taylor to Steve Davis, from John Higgins to Matthew Stevens, from Mark Williams to Ken Doherty, to me – we all admire Jimmy because of his attitude, the way he treats victory and defeat equally.

I once played with him in the Nations Cup in 1999. I felt sorry for him because Stephen Lee, John Parrott and I were all playing brilliantly for England, while Jimmy was playing either OK or awful, and you could see how much he didn't want to let the team down. After we won the tournament we were celebrating with a few drinks. We'd lived through the tournament for a week and won it for England. It was a great victory – England hadn't won for years – but Jimmy was nowhere to be seen. I knew that he felt he hadn't been at his supreme best, so I phoned him and asked him where he was. He said he just felt a bit off-colour. 'Fuck that,' I said to him, 'you were the fucking bollocks, and it was a team effort.' And that was true, because even when Jimmy wasn't playing at his best he still brought up the team spirit. That's the effect he has on other players.

The *News of the World* once did a big story on me and Jimmy out in Thailand. There was a bird – she was called Jim, funnily enough – who was in my room. Believe it or not, she wasn't a prostitute, but I knew everybody else would think she was, and I also knew that a fella from the *News of the World* was around. I knew who the journalists were because I'd been talking to them when I first arrived: they were pretending to be tourists and I was having a nice friendly chat with them when I sussed they were journalists who were looking for the stories on us. So I said, 'Meet me on the twenty-seventh floor and I'll be up there in a minute,' and off she went. Unfortunately, the journalist got in the lift with her and was waiting on the landing when I got up to the twenty-seventh floor myself. I saw both of them and she started calling out my name. I thought, Oh, what the hell, they've got me now, so we just went into the room regardless.

Later they phoned me in the room and asked me if I wanted to comment, and I said, 'Oh, don't do that to me. I'm getting married when I get home and she won't be too happy if she finds out. She won't marry me. Please don't stitch me up.' I couldn't give a shit really, but just thought I'd go along with it for a laugh. It still went in the paper, of course. They ran a classic exclusive: RONNIE IN ROOM WITH BIRD FOR SIX HOURS. Dad was well proud of me. When one of his mates showed him the paper in prison he said, 'That's my boy!' Despite everything, my girlfriend at the time, Vanessa, picked me up from the airport. 'Don't believe everything you read in the papers,' I said, pushing my luck. 'I don't,' she said.

I'd fallen in love with Vanessa, who was about eight years older than me. I met her when I was 18, just after I'd won the UK Championship. I'd only had one bird – Pippa – before, and I certainly wasn't a ladies' man. I was still quite shy. It was Christmas Eve and I'd gone out to a club just after the UK. This blonde bird came in who looked just like Ulrika Jonsson. I started chatting to her and then pestered her for about two months, phoning her at work – she sold the aftershave at Harrods – every day to ask her if I could take her out. She kept saying no because she was already going out with someone, but eventually, she agreed.

We saw each other for a year and a half after that and ended up living together. My mum didn't like her from the beginning because she was so much older than me and still had the boyfriend when we started going out. She wanted a commitment, but there was no way I wanted to have kids back then, so she left me and went travelling to Australia. She ended up having a baby with someone else. I still see her occasionally, and she's certainly a good mum.

The *News of the World* stitched Jimmy up, too, when we were out in Thailand. That really gave me the hump. By the time I was playing in the final Jimmy had left town to face the music. I was with Tony Drago in the foyer of the hotel and spotted the journalist who had written the story. I felt I had to exact some kind of revenge, however pathetic. So I got a big bucket of ice-cold water, went up behind him and poured it over his head. He screamed like a pig. 'That's for stitching up my mate,' I said. 'It doesn't matter about me.' He didn't say anything, but I knew he was shocked. It was as if it had made him think about what he did for a living for the first time. He'd been sent out there purely to stitch people up. It had never happened before, but obviously they knew I was going to be there, Jimmy was going to be there, and they could have some fun.

JOHN PARROTT

When England won the Nations Cup John Parrott was our captain. At the end we jumped over the barrier to give him a big hug because he'd won a good final frame for us.

We're very different characters – John's a family man, into his horse racing, and he doesn't really drink. While Jimmy and I will go out and have fun after an exhibition and end up in all sorts of gaffs, John would rather go out for a meal. But he is good company, especially when we're away in Thailand or China. He'll go out for dinner with us, sit and have a laugh for three or four hours, then he'll go back to the hotel and leave me with Jimmy with a 'Good night, past my bedtime, see you in the morning'. Whenever we're in the Far East, first thing in the morning he'll sit there doing his crosswords. He does the *Times* crossword in about ten minutes. It's a strange mix: one of the lads and then next minute doing the *Times* crossword.

Though I get on well with him, and have been around him for ten years now, I don't really feel I know him. You never get too close to JP. He wouldn't say, 'When you're in Liverpool give me a ring or come over and we'll go for a meal.' It's more likely that he'll see you, ask how you're doing and then he's off. He still plays, of course, but these days he's probably better known for his years on *A Question of Sport* and commentating for the BBC. Quite a few times he's said something that makes me feel uneasy. For instance, he once told me that I've got so much ability, more than he ever had. I don't think he's being fair on himself: he's a great match player, has plenty of bottle, and at one point, before John Higgins, Mark Williams and I came along, he was the only one who'd go toe to toe with Hendry, and he rarely buckled. He was the only one who Stephen didn't like playing.

Another time he suddenly asked how much I'd earned from the game. It wasn't a disrespectful question, he was just interested. I told him and he said, 'Well, I've earned that. True, I've been playing for twice as long but you've got five times my ability.'

I suppose he was paying me a compliment, but it still made me feel bad.

He then said that if I had the head of John Higgins

or Mark Williams I'd never lose. 'There's no one in the world who can get anywhere near you, but sometimes your head goes and then anyone can beat you,' he said.

But *he* certainly knew how to beat me. For a long time, six or seven matches in a row, he was my bogey player and I just couldn't get the better of him.

He had a decent touch, but he used to barge around the table with a tip like a dustbin lid. I once asked him, 'John, how the fuck d'you play with that?'

He just said, 'I stick it on in October and it lasts me through till June.'

I go through a tip every few weeks. I still don't know how he manages to play with the dustbin lid.

STEVE 'THE NUGGET' DAVIS

When I met Steve Davis for the first time, he was already a legend. I was playing in a club in Barking and I'd just lost. Dad said, 'Come on, we'll go home and get a Chinese takeaway.' He phoned up the Chinese and they said, 'Ah Ronnie, Ronnie, we've got David Steven here, David Steven, David Steven.'

'Who's David Steven?' said Dad.

'Snooker player David Steven in the restaurant,' they said.

'Oh, you mean Kirk Stevens?' said Dad.

Del, my coach and mentor on the baize. This was just after coming out of the Priory. I beat Mark Williams in the trial of the Champions Cup. My first win after treatment was a turning point (*Snookerimages/Eric Whitehead*).

Another good night in Ireland,
with Alex Higgins, Del and Jimmy.

OPPOSITE PAGE and ABOVE Scenes from the 2001 World Championship Final; at times the audience were wondering if we were ever going to pot a ball (*all Hulton Getty*).

After winning the world . . . and I'd started out so low at the Crucible (*Tom Jenkins*).

Me, Mum, Jimmy and Ronnie, minutes after winning the
World Championship. I was the calmest one in the room.

The morning after and it still hadn't sunk in
(*Snookerimages/Eric Whitehead*).

ABOVE With Kenny Lynch and a couple of others at a pro-celeb golf tournament; LEFT with my daughter Taylor, indulging in one of my greatest passions; BELOW part of my great run in 2000–2001: winning the Irish Masters (*Snookerimages/Eric Whitehead*).

TOP With Jo, my
girlfriend, meeting
HRH the Duke of
Edinburgh; MIDDLE
at Jimmy White's
daughter's wedding
(with Ronnie Wood);
LEFT Gartree Prison.
It is unusual to be
allowed to take a
photograph in HM's
prisons but an excep-
tion was made after I
won . . .

(Snookerimages/Eric Whitehead)

(Rankin)

'No, David Steven,' they said.

Dad didn't have a clue who they were talking about. We got to the restaurant and Dad said, 'There's a snooker player down here. I don't know for sure who it is, but it might be Kirk Stevens.' In we go and there's the Nugget, Steve Davis.

Dad turned to me and said, 'It's Steve Davis! Go up there and get his autograph.'

'No, I can't,' I said.

'It's all right. You can go and say hello to him. He's eating but he doesn't mind. Just go and ask him.'

So I went up, asked him for his autograph, and he asked me my name. I just about managed to tell him.

'Ah, you're the one who's just had the century break: 117 wasn't it?'

I was gobsmacked. Steve Davis had heard of me. I don't think I got two words out. I couldn't wait to get away from him because I was so scared but also so chuffed. That autograph was my pride and joy. I kept it in my Bible: 'To Ronnie, Best wishes, Steve Davis.'

Dad had his camera with him and took a picture of me and the Nugget. Mum had it enlarged all those years ago and now it hangs in the snooker room at her house alongside my trophies. It's mad looking at the two of us: him the World Champion and nobody knowing that the little boy getting his autograph would play him and go on to become World Champion himself. Steve's even asked for a copy of that photo.

The next time I met him was at Romford Snooker Centre. I must have been around 15, and I went there with a mate of mine, Roy Bacon, just to watch Steve practise. Romford Snooker Centre was called the Matchroom, which was the name of Barry Hearn's company. It was a three-table snooker club: small but plush. Steve's table was out of the way so he didn't get people sitting around as he was practising. When I walked in, he was practising and didn't say anything to me. I went to the toilet for a wee and this fella came in and stood next to me. 'All right, Ronnie. How are you doing?' It was Steve. He started asking me questions about John Higgins: 'Is he a good player?'

'Yeah,' I said, 'a really, really good player.'

We just chatted for a while and when we came out of the toilet he went back to practise.

As we were leaving, I said, 'See you later, Steve.'

A big hand came up. He didn't say anything, just put up his big hand. It was funny the way he did it. That's Steve Davis all over – he's so dry, he's hilarious.

Some time later he asked me down to practise with him. I knew that he wouldn't ask just anybody, so it was an honour. It was so serious, just like playing in a televised match, and there was no chatting this time. He just asked if I wanted a cup of tea, and that was it. I think he beat me 5–3, which I was delighted with. He was number two in the world at the time but I still gave him too much respect. He's a great player, but at the time I credited him with being even better than he was. He wasn't unbeatable, but in my mind he was a god, and I found it difficult in front of him, desperate to prove to him that I was a good player.

Whenever I met Steve, I was in awe of him. Whereas with Jimmy I felt comfortable, I worried about every little thing with Steve. I was always on my best behaviour in case he didn't ask me back to practise with him again. But now that I know Steve I realise I shouldn't have worried. You can have a laugh and joke when you're playing snooker with him. It's not all serious, but he just comes across that way. He became ironically known as Steve 'Interesting' Davis as a joke because people thought he was dull, and he plays on that name now, but he's not boring at all. He *is* interesting to talk to and to be around. I've had some great nights when I've gone out with the Nugget for a meal and just talked about snooker. (By the way, he's called the Nugget because he had the golden touch.) In the early days I'd ask him questions like 'What's running side, what are reverse side and check side?' He'd look at me as if I were mad, as if I were winding him up. A snooker player should know that stuff but I didn't – I just knew about right-hand side or left-hand side. Eventually he'd tell me, and I knew he thought I was playing stupid, but I wasn't.

That's one of the things I like most about the Nugget: you can get on to snooker with him and he'll always have something interesting to say. Everything he says about the game is worth listening to.

The Nugget never really gets as much credit as he

deserves for his ingenuity: he invented so many shots in snooker. There's one where the red is off the side cushion and you're in trouble off the break, and he'd come off one cushion, cannon into the red, and leave the white safe on the bottom cushion. Before he came up with that, players felt they had no option but to take on the red and it often cost them the frame. It was because he was such a good billiards player that he could play shots like that. I started playing that shot myself, although not nearly as well as he played it. It wasn't a trick shot, like John Virgo or Dennis Taylor play – this was not only an ingenious shot, it was a potentially frame-saving shot.

The Nugget practised like a maniac. He was obsessed with playing. I heard stories that he would go to the club and hit the cue ball up and down the middle of the table for two hours just to make sure he was hitting it in the middle. He knows the technique side of the game inside out. Perhaps that was his downfall because he became so much of a perfectionist that in the end he didn't know what he was doing. He reached a point where at every tournament he would have a different cue action. At one point he said he was going to cue up like me! When he said that I thought he was taking the piss because I was struggling with my game so much at the time and I hated the way that I cued. I just wanted to cue like Steve Davis!

A little while later I was playing him in a tournament and I could see just what he was doing: he was pulling his arm through on the shot and dropping it, like I do. He had said in a newspaper, 'I've seen Ronnie O'Sullivan play and that's why he gets through the ball so well, because he has such a good follow-through.' But I thought that was a flaw in my technique, something I've tried to eradicate over the years. I couldn't believe he was serious, but he was. At that point I knew he'd come unstuck. For him, the game had become too technical.

Snooker has changed so much over the years. Steve is only in his mid-40s, and years ago a great player could just be coming into his prime at that age, and could go on as a champion for decades. Not any more, though. With the way Steve Davis plays the game, he's good enough to survive in the modern era, but he's a little too negative to be a winner. Nowadays he'll have a chance to pot the blue and go into the pack, and he will go into them, but he won't try to smash the balls all over the table. He invented that shot and usually it would be a frame-winner. I think if he were to play more like that today he'd still be a force.

Some of the best snooker that's been played against me was played by Steve Davis in 1997, when he beat me in the Benson and Hedges final. I was 8–4 up and went into the dressing room at the interval rubbing my hands together – there was no way the Nugget could beat me now. I only needed two more frames. He beat me 10–8 and I didn't get a shot.

I don't think he takes his career as a player too seriously now. Mind you, as I was writing this, he surprised everyone by getting through to the semi-final of the LG Cup in Preston, only to be narrowly beaten by Alan McManus. He's more interested in making a career away from the table. He might win another tournament, but deep down I think he's accepted that he won't be competing at the very top level, and his future probably lies in the commentating that he's started doing. Perhaps he'll end up as the new Ted Lowe.

ALEX 'HURRICANE' HIGGINS

The first time I met the Hurricane was in Barking. Alex Higgins was a legend, but he was more my dad's generation than mine: when he was at his peak I was tiny. I met him in 1986, four years after he won his last World Championship – the famous one when he brought his wife and baby on stage and cried in front of the cameras. And by now, he was getting well past his best, but he was still a hero, and when he turned up he looked fit and healthy. He had style.

He was doing an exhibition, and the manager of the club said I could give him a frame. I was one of about ten who played him that day in front of hundreds of his fans. I had on my little dickie-bow and my shirt. I was only about 10. I made a 20 break against him and was a bit gutted that I didn't pot a few more balls (it was around that time when I started making breaks of 100).

He always had a thing for cues: he liked to change his all the time. Everyone loved my cue: it was really old, a beautiful bit of wood, and everybody who picked it up commented on the balance, the feel, the touch it gave you. Dad said, 'If he comes anywhere near your cue, tell me, because he ain't having it.'

I next met him when I was 16 in Blackpool, in my first season as a professional. I played all my qualifying matches and then six weeks later Alex had to come up to play his. I went to watch his games because I wanted to see if he was still any good, and how he played. I'd heard so much about him and I wanted to see it for myself. I sat in the front row and watched his mannerisms. He used to walk back to his chair, head nodding like a chicken, and stare at me as if I'd done something wrong. I thought, Has he got the hump with me? Should I get up and go? Am I putting him off? Finally he mumbled, 'Go and get me a Guinness. Get me a Guinness!'

So I ran out and got him a Guinness.

From then on I watched all his matches and I was like his little mascot. Every match he would say, 'Go and get me a Guinness, Ronnie, and half a lager. Half a lager and a Guinness.' He slurred his words so they all ran into one.

I thought, This is blinding, I'm getting Alex Higgins's drinks for him. I was so chuffed that he asked me and didn't ask anybody else. I'd take the drinks back and watch him.

Len Ganley was refereeing him once, and he said to Len, 'Stand back.'

Len replied, 'I am standing back, Alex.'

Alex said, 'Stand back two paces.'

Len said, 'I am standing back two paces.'

'You're a big man, Len, you're a big man,' said Alex.

He hated Len Ganley, but the officials always made Len or John Williams referee Alex's matches, because they knew that Alex would frighten the life out of any other referee. I've seen it myself: he does intimidate people.

Now I know him, I think he just wants approval. He loves the attention and the buzz. He loves to show off and entertain. That first time when he'd stared at me and I'd been worried sick he was just looking at me for approval, silently asking me whether he looked good.

Years later in Dublin I'd just won the Benson and Hedges Irish Masters. Alex came up to me and said, 'Ronnie, I can make you win the World.'

'What are you on about, Alex?' I said.

'I'll come to Sheffield with you and I will make you win the World Championship.'

'Fucking hell, Alex,' I said. 'You're having a laugh, aren't you? I've got my man here, Del. He's my coach. He goes everywhere with me.'

'Who's that then?' said Alex.

'Him there,' I said, 'that's Del.'

He looked at Del, all six foot eight of him. He gave him the once over and said in that lispy mumble of his, part Brando, part street dosser, 'You're so tall you could stick the black on the spot from the yellow end.'

I thought he'd gone nuts. Del just started laughing.

One night in Dublin a call came through to my room. I was in bed asleep and my mate Mickey the Mullet was in the next bed to mine. He answered the phone and asked who it was.

'It's Alex.'

'Alex, it's half three in the morning,' said Mickey.

'Tell Ronnie I want three minutes of his time.'

'What do you want three minutes of his time for?' asked Mickey. 'To boil an egg?'

I'd woken up by this stage and was lying there laughing my bollocks off.

'Nah,' said Alex. 'Tell him there's a good party to go to. There's loads of women and loads of booze.'

'Alex,' said Mickey, 'we're not interested, we're trying to get some sleep.'

'Well, can you give Ronnie a message?'

'What's that then?'

'Tell him to fuck off.'

PETER EBDON

My dad nicknamed Peter Ebdon 'Psycho'. The first time I met him was at King's Cross Snooker Centre. He was about 14 years old, so I would have been 8.

He had short hair and was quite skinny, and he had these mad, intense eyes.

'He doesn't look a bad player does he?' said Dad. So he went up to him and said, 'Do you want to give my boy a game?'

I played Peter for three or four hours and Dad asked him if he'd be down there the next week. Peter said he would, so Dad said, 'Great, I'll bring my boy down every Saturday for a game.'

Soon after we met I went away with him and Dad to Hemsby, near Great Yarmouth. In the car on the way down there Peter was asleep with his suitcase on top of him and his arms folded around it. His mum must have told him to keep an eye on his gear, make sure none of us messed around, as he hardly knew us. When we arrived in Hemsby Dad asked if he could borrow Peter's comb. Peter handed it over, but later I saw him soaking it in Dettol. I guess his mum must have told him not to let anyone use his comb because you don't know what they've got.

I grew up with Peter, and I've had a lot of matches with him when he's totally lost the plot. I played him in a Pro-Am in Witham – one of those where you get there at ten in the morning, have your bacon sarnie, and then play six or seven matches, best of five all day, and they go on till one or two the next morning. Peter was a serial winner, coming out on top in Pro-Am after Pro-Am. Apart from Anthony Hamilton, there was no one to touch him. I must have been 13 or 14 when I drew Peter in the semi-finals. He used to turn up in dickie-bow, wing-collar shirt, cufflinks and waistcoat, while everyone else was in jeans and a T-shirt. He was a character. He'd stand there not giving a fuck what anyone thought of him. I think that's great. He's his own person.

At Witham in the semis I was 2–1 up and he needed snookers in the fourth frame. I potted a ball, then another, and I was getting faster and faster around the table. He shouted, 'Go on, Jimmy. Go on, Jimmy!' And I thought, He's enjoying this, so I started lamping them in from everywhere, playing one-handed, all sorts of stuff. After the match he was pacing up and down the club, and then he came up to me and said, 'You're a good player, but you'll never, ever, beat me again.'

'You've gone,' I said. 'I've done you. Your head has totally gone. For you to come out with that I must be totally in your head.' And it was true.

Peter's brother-in-law told a mate of mine, 'We came out of that snooker club and we were meant to be heading south and we ended up heading north fifty miles before he realised where he was going. Ronnie must have done his head in big style.'

To give Peter his due, the next time I played him at Witham, about two months later, he beat me. I went 1–0 up and really wanted to slaughter him to rub it in. He won the next three frames. I hated losing at the best of times, but I was really gutted that time.

He came up to me afterwards, shook my hand and said, 'What I said the other day, I was out of order. You're better than Ken Doherty and James Wattana.

You're the best player I've played against.' Ken and James had just turned pro at the time. I was only 14 and I thought it was great that he could say he was in the wrong rather than carrying a grudge.

Since then I've usually got the better of him on a snooker table. I had to play him in Aberdeen once and I was asked how I felt about playing Peter in the next round. 'Who?' I said. 'The Psycho?' The reporters started laughing and writing down the nickname. Peter must have seen it on Teletext in his room because I was sitting in the restaurant eating my grub and he came running through the door shouting, 'Am I a psycho, then? Am I? Am I a psycho?' He was terrifying. If I hadn't known him so well I would have thought I had really upset him this time.

'Look at you,' I said. 'You're completely nuts. You're just round the fucking bend, aren't you?'

And he started laughing, even though his eyes were still all Anthony Perkins. He might be totally mental, but he's a nice mental. You can have a laugh with him.

He's also very, very bright and one of the most genuine blokes on the snooker circuit. If you win a tournament, he's the first to congratulate you. If you play well against him, he'll come off the table and say, 'You played brilliantly.' He doesn't like losing, but he's not a bad loser – if he thinks he deserved to be beaten, he'll say the best man won on the day.

The only thing I don't like about him is the way he punches the air after he's won. You've just been beaten, which is horrible, and he goes around punching the air. But when he won the World Championship in 2002 he held himself together well, he didn't punch the air. I was watching it with my girlfriend Jo, and whenever anybody rang I said, 'Make sure you see it because if it's Peter who wins, he's going to go mental. He's capable of doing anything.' Then when he won it and was so calm I couldn't believe it. But I thought, Brilliant, good on you. I was so glad he'd won, and even more happy that he held it all in, because the last thing you want to see when you've just lost a huge match is someone running round like a lunatic.

I thought there was no way in the world he could beat Stephen Hendry over two days in that final. But then I didn't expect him to beat Anthony Hamilton so easily in the quarters, and I really didn't expect him to beat Matthew Stevens in the semis. I think he'll admit himself that the semi-final was his hardest match at Sheffield, and that Matthew should have won – Psycho won a lot of frames he had no right to win. But that is why he's such a tough opponent. Peter never knows when he's beaten. And that's one of the essential qualities of most World Champions. His mental strength and his desire are such huge assets. When he gets something in his head, like he wanted to win that World Championship, it takes something really special to beat him. Even if he is five frames down, he'll still be giving it his all. When I'm in that position, I usually just decide to have a laugh, but Peter is so intense he'll just keep going.

MARK WILLIAMS

I grew up with Mark on the junior circuit and through the Pro-Am days. He's about a year older than me. Although he lived in Wales and I was in Essex, we would see each other regularly because of snooker. We turned professional at the same time in Blackpool in 1992. Neither of us could drive, but Dad used to let us take his Mercedes round Norbreck Castle car park. I remember Mark telling Dad it was a blinding motor.

'You'll have one of these one day,' said Dad.

'No, I won't have one of them,' he said. Mark thought he'd never be able to afford one.

But of course Dad was right and he went on to have a lot of success. I think he's changed over the years, though. I find him difficult to get on with now. He's a bit of a Jekyll and Hyde character with me: one minute he says hello, the next he's blanking me.

After he beat Jimmy in the Benson and Hedges in 2002 I congratulated him. Jimmy had beaten me in the quarter-finals, and there were so many people backing him that it was one of the toughest matches I've ever played in. Mark beat Jimmy 6–5 and I said to him, 'I take my hat off to you, well played, because I found it fucking hard with that crowd rooting for Jimmy, so well done.' He seemed to appreciate the compliment. But after that he won a couple of tournaments and started blanking me again. I had no idea where I stood with him.

We often used to practise together, and we had an understanding when we were kids. Later, it bothered me that I found it difficult to connect with Mark. I'd ask myself why he acted the way he did, but the only reason I could think of was that he was winning tournaments and there was some kind of mind games going on. For instance, he'd take ages to look down a pot to see if it went and you'd think, Well, obviously it doesn't go or it must be very tight. Eventually he'd get down and just smash it in easy as anything.

It might sound trivial, but those are exactly the kinds of things that can affect you in a snooker match. Mark's attitude, both on and off the table, doesn't bother me now because I feel comfortable in myself. If that's what he feels he has to do, then that's what he's got to do ...

JOHN HIGGINS

John Higgins is the nicest person you could ever meet. He's one of the most genuine people I've come across. The first time I played him was in the Home Internationals when I was 14. We were in the junior event, and nobody had heard of John. It was Mark Williams and me who were supposedly the two best youngsters on the scene. Scotland were playing Wales, and somebody told me that this Scottish kid called John Higgins had almost had a 147: he'd had eleven reds and eleven blacks. The name didn't mean a thing to me.

Then I played him in the quarter-finals of the junior competition at Prestatyn, and I knew I wouldn't forget his name – he beat me 2–1. One of my mates asked him if it was a good game and, so my mate told me, John said, 'Yeah, it was all right, but that Ronnie O'Sullivan's got no bottle.' Looking back on it now, I think my mate was probably winding me up, because I could never imagine John saying something like that – it's not in his character.

We have never been out drinking much. He likes a little drink, but on the whole when he's at tournaments he's very serious and focused, a true professional. That's what I admire about him. And if he's playing well there's nothing you can do but sit in your chair: he goes on missions when he just doesn't miss.

I played him in the Matchroom League once. Before the match I saw Jimmy White and he said to me, 'Where were you last night?'

'What d'you mean?'

'Me and John went out to this little pub and watched the football, and Higgins got slaughtered.'

I thought, Aye, aye, that'll do nicely, he won't be able to pot a ball today. John was sitting there reading the paper. He didn't look too bad, but he didn't look too well, either.

I had a 40 break in the first frame, and he came to the table and cleared up. Then he had a 100, then a 90, then another 100. This was after he'd been out on the piss all night. He didn't miss a ball. He can't have gone out last night, I thought. There's no way that anyone can play like that with a hangover.

At the interval he said to me, 'I can't stop shaking, we were drinking so much last night,' having just played some of the best snooker I've ever seen.

At the World Championship in 1998 he played another session against me when I didn't pot a ball. It was 4–4, and he just wiped the floor with me to go 12–4 up. The final match score was 17–10. He hammered me. I was lucky to get ten frames. I knew he was going to win the World that year. Del had said to me, 'I fancy you this year, we're going to win here,' but I didn't feel confident, didn't feel good about myself, and John just stuffed me, I didn't have any answers. He was completely on top of his game, and although I was playing OK I knew I wasn't playing well enough to beat him.

Without a doubt the best player I've ever played against is Stephen Hendry (more about him in a second) but John Higgins is a close second (followed by Mark Williams, Steve Davis and then Jimmy White). The one difference between them is that, with Hendry, when you've left the table you can never be totally sure that you've played a good enough safety shot. John plays more of a percentage game. In a way, though, that makes him harder to beat because his safety game is so brilliant.

STEPHEN HENDRY

At the time of writing I have just seen Stephen Hendry for the first time since I announced I wanted to beat him up badly and send him back down the motorway in the 2002 World Championship. We have just played in the Scottish Masters in Glasgow, the first tournament of the 2002–3 season, which I won – a great feeling. I beat Stephen in the semis, and then John Higgins in the final. Stephen and I shook hands before the match but he refused to talk to me. I saw him outside the hall, gave him a big hello, but he ignored me. I half wanted to say, 'Look, I didn't really mean what I said, I was just trying to spice up the match,' but that wouldn't have been quite true. I *did* want to beat him up, but I hope Stephen knew that I meant on the snooker table rather than physically. Maybe I should have made it more obvious, there was a lot of frustration surfacing; perhaps my lifetime's frustration in snooker was expressed in that moment.

There'd been tension between us since I'd played Stephen at the World Championship in 1999. If your opponent thinks you've missed a ball deliberately when you're snookered, he can ask you to play it again. That's what Stephen asked me to do, and I thought he was out of order. He knows that I've never missed a ball deliberately. It's just not how I play the game. I've never come out of a match so wound up. It seemed like such bad sportsmanship to me and I lost a lot of respect for him because of it. That was a real shame because that semi-final was one of the best matches anybody has seen on the telly. Hendry beat me 17–14. He had four or five centuries, and I had four, on one of which I missed the pink for a 147 when I was on 134. That would have been my second maximum at Sheffield, which nobody's managed up to now, and I'd loved to have done it.

The memory of that semi-final had festered for three years and in 2002 I thought, Yes, this is payback time. In the end it wasn't, of course. It backfired on me, and I lost. Maybe I should have controlled myself in front of the cameras in that interview, but I wanted to say it so I said it.

The frustration with Stephen goes much deeper than that match in 1999, though. At its heart was what I had to put up with when Ian Doyle managed both of us. I don't think Ian likes me now. He hasn't spoken to me since my outburst before playing Stephen in 2002. Perhaps that's because he has a father–son relationship with Stephen, like I had a father–son relationship with Barry Hearn. He finds it personally insulting and hurtful if anybody stands up to Stephen or if anybody criticises him. With Ian, Stephen was always the number one, and got the top treatment. He got the car to drive him to the match, whereas the rest of us had to take courtesy cars. If Stephen was doing anything, he'd always be driven by John Carroll. The rest of us in Ian's stable used to have a laugh about it because it was so blatant –

the car would draw up, and we'd say, 'Oh, here it is, the car for Lord Hendry.'

There was an incident in the 1999 semi-final that I think explains how the Ian Doyle stable worked. It came at the point when I was tied 12–12 with Hendry, and just about to go into the final session. I walked into the restaurant at the hotel, and John Carroll was sitting down with Ian Doyle. I was with my mate Andrew, who had come up for the tournament as my corner man, and we were waiting for a table when Ian called me over.

'Listen, Ronnie, you've not got any holidays booked, have you?' he said.

'No, I've got no holidays booked.'

'Good. Because if you win the World Championship you're going to be in untold demand, there are going to be press people who'll be desperate to grab hold of you, there'll be sponsors. There'll be this and that.'

'Ian,' I said, 'I don't want to know about this. I'm in the middle of the biggest match of my life. The last thing I want to do is start thinking ahead about all these wonderful contracts that I'm going to be offered. I don't want to talk about that. I'm just here to play a fucking snooker match.'

Some people have suggested that Ian Doyle's only in snooker for the money and that he doesn't even like the game. I don't think that's true. He does love the game, and he loves Stephen Hendry. By the time I signed for Doyle, when I was 21, I knew how to drive a hard bargain. The deal I struck meant I had far more control over my income than did most represented players. But I didn't like the way he treated me, and I hated it when he wanted to set up his own tour. To do that, in effect he had to dismantle the game as it was. I made a deal with the World Snooker Association to stay with them because I wanted an out from Ian anyway, and it was probably the best move I've ever made because it made me my own person again.

With the way it was in Ian's stable, I knew if I was up against one of his big three, he'd be rooting for them. It was a crazy situation, really, and I think the word 'stable' says it all. Could you imagine Alex Ferguson managing Manchester United, Liverpool and Arsenal at the same time? To me, the idea of the snooker stable seems to be both degrading and an obvious conflict of interest.

In December 2000 I finally split from Doyle. I didn't want to be second to anybody else. I was at the stage in my career where I needed to be his priority. Since then I've played some of my best snooker. I won the Benson and Hedges Irish Masters just after I left him, then the World Championship and the Premier League. That was all very nice, especially as I beat Stephen Hendry in two finals – the Irish Masters and the Premier League. I have come out on top more often than not in my games with Stephen. And I'm very proud of that record.

People ask me what Stephen Hendry is really like? I think he can be a bit boring sometimes, but he's not nasty. He's really focused and just gets on with the job, it's just that he's quite shy, not a very good conversationalist.

Years ago, when Stephen had just beaten me in the Benson and Hedges final, Ian Doyle was standing next to Del when we were doing our post-match interviews. Ian said to Del in front of everybody, 'For Ronnie to be like Stephen, he's got to be—'

Del just cut him off before he'd finished. He said, 'Whoa, whoa, whoa, Ian. We don't want Ronnie to be like Stephen. Ronnie puts bums on seats.'

Yet for all my feelings about Stephen, he is in my mind probably the greatest snooker player there has ever been. What makes him the best is his potting under pressure. Any good player can pot balls, but he can pot them best when the pressure is really on. He always produces his best form in the most pressured situation, usually the World Championship. And just when you think you've got him safe, he'll pot a red and make a hundred off it. Sometimes his shot selection seems to be verging on the suicidal, but often enough – too often for the rest of us – he makes the pot. So the shots aren't suicidal at all: they're his version of a calculated risk. Under pressure, he goes up a gear, whereas most players usually go down one. His long potting is also consistently the best in the game.

All these things are why I say that he is arguably the best ever.

CHAPTER ELEVEN

Becoming World Champion

It was nearly a year since I'd been in the Priory, and although I was still on the Twelve-Step Programme and looking after myself physically, I wasn't feeling any better mentally. If anything, I was feeling worse. Not drinking and not puffing was a step in the right direction, but no real cure for my depression. Things reached rock bottom just before the World Championship in 2001. It had got to the point where I couldn't face people. Shortly before Sheffield I went to Aberdeen to play in a tournament, and I had three TVs in my room – one for my PlayStation, one for my video and the one that the hotel supplied – so I did not need to come out of my room except to play snooker.

Occasionally, Del would go downstairs and say to one of the players – maybe Jimmy White or Stephen Hendry – 'D'you fancy going up and having a game of Golf with Ronnie on the PlayStation.' So they'd come up for an hour to my room to play. I'd have my food brought up to me. I'd leave my room half an hour before my match to hit a few balls and then I'd go to play the game.

I ended up winning that Aberdeen tournament,

but I was still in bits. A lot of the players who had known me when I was an amateur said I'd changed. I'd get shirty and defensive, and tell them I didn't know what they meant about me not being the same person. But they were right. I'd lost my sense of humour and my ease with people. They'd be chatting to me and I'd be millions of miles away. I couldn't understand what people were saying, couldn't follow the simplest conversations. It was as if fear had paralysed my brain.

Yet from the outside it looked as though I had everything. I was a good snooker player with a nice house, a car to drive around in, and took holidays all over the world. Why wouldn't you be happy if you had all that? I couldn't work out what was wrong with me, and I was always searching for something different that would make me happy. There were times when I thought if I gave up snooker and ran the business for Dad I would be happy. I would have been working in the shops as well as outside pulling the strings. I think I would have done it all right; it was something I could have fitted into easily. Ultimately I'm glad I stuck with the snooker, and went through the bad times … and have come out the other end.

But the bad times were *really* bad: even when I was winning it wasn't fun. It was just a big pay cheque. Hip-hip-hurray! I'd already won four tournaments that season and hadn't got a buzz from winning any of them. I told myself I had a choice to be happy and skint or miserable with a few quid in my pocket. Snooker provided the money, but I was convinced that snooker was the problem. It wasn't, of course. The problem was my head.

Just before Sheffield I felt empty. A week before the tournament started I went into the club to practise with Anthony Hamilton, who I've known for years, since we played in the Pro-Ams. I played four or five frames, and put my cue away.

'Ant, I can't play any more.'

'I can see that,' he said and asked what was wrong.

I couldn't tell him. I just said, 'I'm sorry about wasting your day.'

I went home and told Mum I didn't want to play the game any more. I told her Sheffield would be my last tournament.

Del said we should go to the doctor to see if he could get me on tablets. I went, but at first I wouldn't talk to the doctor. Then I opened up: I explained that I couldn't get off the settee because I didn't have any enthusiasm for anything – didn't talk, couldn't sleep, couldn't think, wasn't interested in sex, didn't feel good about anything.

'You suffer with depression,' said Dr Hodges. It wasn't the first time I'd heard this, but I felt I really had to do something about it this time. He told me about how we create the chemical serotonin, and how we need it to give us energy and make ourselves feel good. He said that if normal people are usually at a level of ten, and on a bad day they will go down to nine, then I was at a level of three or four. He said there is something in my brain that's breaking down the serotonin every time it wants to do its job. 'I'm going to put you on these pills that make serotonin and they will make you function like a normal human being again,' he told me. It made sense to me, but I still didn't think there was any way it could make me feel better. He told me that it would take about eleven days for it to start working.

I'd tried Prozac once before, but had given up after three days – which was mad. This time he said if I went on it I had to give it a proper go. 'When you get to level two or three that is suicidal. I think you're on three or three and a half,' he told me again to hammer home the point. I didn't know whether he was saying all this just so that I'd take the pills, but it did make sense to me because I knew how I was feeling. I thought, Well, yeah, I do want to kill myself. All that was stopping me was that I didn't have the bottle. There were times when I just didn't want to live, but suicide takes serious bottle. I thought about how I would do it. I couldn't stab myself, I couldn't shoot myself, I'm scared of heights so I wouldn't want to jump off a building. If I smashed the car up I might survive and be a cabbage in a wheelchair, and that would just top everything off!

'I have thought about killing myself,' I told the doctor, 'but I know I haven't got the bottle to do it.' I didn't go into any more detail.

I'd said it to Mum and Dad before, and had said it to myself on a regular basis. I know it devastated Mum and Dad when I talked like that. Now that I feel more positive and I hear people talk like that I think, You're having a laugh, aren't you? Things could never be that bad. But then I think back and realise, yes, they *can* be that bad. That's how I was. I felt worthless, useless. I just wanted to fuck everything off and run away. I didn't enjoy the life I had playing snooker and I couldn't see a way out. What it boiled down to was not being able to relax or have a laugh. I'd become so negative and so stiff, and I longed to change my personality. I wanted to be a funny, carefree person. I was depressed, of course, but stupidly I thought that could be put right if I was able to start smoking dope again.

When the doctor explained about serotonin it made me feel a bit better: that it wasn't just me being weird and pathetic; that there was a chemical reason for the way I was feeling. He said the pills would help me, but if I didn't want to start taking them now that was OK – I could wait till after the tournament. That seemed to make sense, so for the time being help was at hand but I wasn't going to use it immediately.

I flew to Manchester to do *A Question of Sport*. I've often shied away from doing programmes like that, even though I'm always asked, because I've always known that I couldn't cope with these 'fun' experiences. This time was no exception. After the show I didn't even go to the green room for the after-show hospitality. And let's face it, Sue Barker, John Parrott, Ally McCoist and co. register pretty high in the nice people stakes. Instead I went back to my hotel room and sulked, while Del made the Horlicks.

Next stop was the Crucible for the World Championship. On the opening Saturday at Sheffield I phoned the Samaritans. Even by my standards I was a wreck. I thought people who are depressed phone the Samaritans, so that's what I did. The woman on the phone said, 'You're welcome to come down to our place in Sheffield and have a chat with our people,' but the World Championship was the only thing going on in Sheffield at the time, and the last thing I wanted was to be in the paper for sitting down and having a chat with the Samaritans.

I never told them my name. I said I was a sportsman who played snooker, and that I'd been having panic attacks, suffering anxiety, when I got out of bed in the morning I couldn't face people, I had a lot of fear in me, I didn't want to play snooker any more.

The girl at the other end of the line said, 'Do you *have* to play snooker?'

'Well, it's my life,' I said. 'It's what I do for my job. I want to be able to play.'

'Isn't it more important for you to be healthy?' she said. 'Have you ever thought of giving up snooker?'

'Yeah, I have thought about giving up snooker – for the last eight years,' I said. 'But I haven't done so yet. I'm trying to be a little realistic here. And the thought of me not playing snooker any more right now is not realistic.'

I felt better by talking to her. I had nothing to hide on the phone. The worst thing for me was talking to people who didn't know how I was feeling and having to put on this big front that I was all right. If I told people on the circuit that I was really depressed, or told them I was having a panic attack and couldn't be around them, they'd look at me as if I were completely mad.

But there was no hiding how I felt from everyone. Things had come to a head on the radio. The press officer at the World Championship had asked me to do an interview on that Saturday morning. 'No problem,' I said. He said they'd ring me at 9.30 a.m., get me ready on the line, and do a live link-up from my room. The phone rang. 'Ronnie, you're on line with us. How are you doing?'

'Fine,' I said. 'Feeling good,' which was completely not the case. But that was my stock response: making out that everything was hunky-dory. I'd always thought if anybody asks you how you are, you say you're feeling good – people don't really want to hear about all your problems. I'd been saying it for so many years when I felt terrible, but I thought if I told them how I really felt they'd probably start crying or running away. I didn't want to put people on a downer.

So I got chatting to this fella, who told me that I would be doing an interview with a woman. He said, 'Just wait for thirty seconds and you'll be live on air.'

A few seconds went by and then this woman's voice asked me how I was feeling about Sheffield.

'Yeah, looking forward to it,' I said. 'Had a good season so far,' blah, blah, blah. I felt like I was blabbering on, telling complete lies. It didn't feel right. I thought, I'm coming out with a load of garbage here. And suddenly I just couldn't do it any more: I broke out and told her how I really felt: 'I don't want to play the game no more. I feel ill with it. I'm not looking forward to this tournament one little bit. I actually can't wait till it's over. The only thing I'm happy about is that it's my last competitive tournament and then I've got three months when I don't even have to think about it. I'm just not up for it at all.'

'Oh,' she said. Her tone of voice had changed. She'd gone from the professional, bouncy interviewer to somebody who just felt sorry for me and was wishing me the best. 'I hope you feel better, Ronnie, and I wish you well,' she said.

'Thank you very much,' I said.

Then a fella came on the line and said, 'Yeah, we all wish you well, Ronnie. Just stick in there and we hope you're feeling better.'

As soon as I'd said all of that I felt a huge weight had been lifted. Instead of pretending everything was OK I was finally telling people how I felt. It was therapeutic. Until then, Del was the only person I'd felt I could be honest with, without it being spread around the circuit and everybody asking, 'What's up with Ronnie?'

Del was just sitting there in the room next to me, rigid. I could see he was thinking, Oh, what has he said now? But Del would never say, 'You shouldn't have done that'; he's not one of those people. He gave me a big cuddle and said everything was going to be all right.

'But Del, I feel so terrible,' I said.

'You are a depressive. I've spoken to people, and they all say that. Your doctor told you the same thing. Get this tournament out of the way, we'll get you on these pills, and I believe you are going to be well again. You've got an illness, and it's nothing to be ashamed of.'

I said, 'Del, I don't care. I've tried everything there is to try – psychiatrists, therapists, the Priory, this, that and the other – and I still feel like shit.' I didn't know where to turn. I'd had it with psychotherapists.

In my first match at Sheffield I had an easy win against Andy Hicks, but I was a total mess inside. Afterwards I realised that, Sheffield or no Sheffield, I couldn't go another day feeling like this. I was at my wit's end and thought Prozac was the only hope. I said to Del, 'If we've got to go back to London to get this prescription, let's do it.'

'Let me phone your doctor,' he said, 'and we'll see if we can get him to send the prescription up here to save us going all the way back there. But you're sure you want it?'

'I'm positive,' I said. 'Snooker is the least important thing to me at the moment. The most important thing is if there's something out there that can help me, I want it. I'd go to the other end of the world for it.' I was feeling rock bottom. I would try anything.

Del reminded me about what the doctor had said

about it making me sick, dizzy and high, and that it could well affect my form. 'Fuck the snooker. I just want to try these pills out. If they do work, I want some of it.' I was desperate, and I was finally putting my health in front of my snooker. It could well have cost me the World Championship that year if I'd had a funny trip halfway through a match, but I reckoned happiness and stability were more important to me.

When I first started taking Prozac it made me feel really dizzy. I started taking it in the second round against Dave Harold. At the World Championship second-round matches are played over twenty-five frames split into three sessions. The worst time for me was between noon and three in the afternoon because that was when the rush of these tablets hit me for the first time. They made me feel so chilled, so stress-free, but physically I couldn't play snooker. It was just this period that was tricky for me, and then I felt fine.

The little buzz from the pills was great. I thought, This is how I want to be feeling all the time. OK, I might not be able to play snooker, but I no longer feel that I'm carrying the whole world on my shoulders.

During the match against Dave, Willie Thorne was commentating and he said, 'Ronnie doesn't look interested.' I didn't feel good, but for some reason I was winning – not in style, but doing the job. When I watched the highlights Willie said that I was going for shots that I shouldn't be going for, but at the end of the session he said, 'Well he's ten–six up now, and I can't see him losing from this position.' You could almost hear Willie's brain ticking over. 'Hold on a minute,' he said, 'I've just said he's been playing shots he shouldn't be going for, but he's had 88, 96, 104, 110, 54, 62, 48, and that is frighteningly high-scoring snooker. And we think he's not been playing that well, and doesn't look interested.'

The thing is, I *was* playing poorly, and not executing the shots how I wanted to, but they were still going in the holes and I was making 80s and 90s from nowhere, so I was doing something right. I was back to being a human being. That's what the Prozac must have done – it made me realise that a win is a win whether it's pretty or not, whether I look as if I'm interested or I don't. Steve Davis once said you should play snooker as if it means everything but it means nothing. It's not an easy balance to achieve, but in the second round I felt I was getting there. The worry had gone and I won 13–6.

In the quarter-finals I played Peter Ebdon over two days, the first day being a morning and an evening session. I came out of the morning session with Peter 4–4. You play sixteen sessions in the World Championship if you win the tournament, and I didn't lose one session that year. The worst result was that 4–4 against Peter. I could never understand it when people said, 'Just play one session at a time.' But since taking Prozac I've understood exactly what they mean.

After the 4–4 session Del was saying, 'Re-sult! Re-sult!'

'Do you think so?' I said.

'Of course. He can't play any better. Peter Ebdon has flown out of his nut, and you've stuck with him, and made a ton to tie up the match. He probably feels he should be six–two up, and perhaps he should be, but you battled. That's the best match snooker I've seen you play.'

I wasn't convinced. 'D'you think so?' I repeated.

'Ron, a week ago I'd be in here now having to pick you up from being seven–one or six–two down, but you battled, and I'm so proud of you. Trust me.'

After the morning session I had my tablet and the buzz came on me, but luckily I didn't have to play then. By the evening it had worn off, and I won the session 8–0. So I'd won nine frames on the spin, and was 12–4 up.

One of the crunch frames was when I was 10–4 up. Peter was on a break of 64, and he went for a mad shot to try to make a 147 – he'd taken eight reds and eight blacks. He missed and I cleared the table. When I saw him play that shot, I knew mentally he was gone, because he would normally have ignored it. Even though there was a chance of a 147, the most important thing is to win the frame. I reckoned at that point he'd thrown in the towel and was thinking, I know I'm not going to win the match, but I'll try to get a 147 out of it and nick 150 grand. That was the prize money on offer for a maximum break. I buzzed off it and won the last frame of the session, too.

I'd had my wits about me, but the final session was in the afternoon, when I felt at my ropiest. As soon as I started playing, my whole body was shaking. I couldn't really see and I had no feeling in my body. Peter Ebdon is mentally one of the hardest players to put away because he never knows when he's beaten. Even at 12–4, you know he'll come out and play as if it's 0–0. Peter won the first two frames, and I thought, Here we go, but then I thought, Wait a minute. I'm 12–4 up. It was a massive lead and even if I'd been hopping round on one leg, or using one hand, the chances were that I could get a 50 or 60 break and win the single frame I needed. It was probably the Prozac that gave me the new calm and optimism. And that optimism gave me the mental strength to get on with the task – putting in a champion's performance on the table. I ended up beating Peter 13–6, and by the end I thanked God I'd got over the line because I felt a bit wobbly.

My mood was transformed in Sheffield. On Prozac, I would wake up and think, Today's not a bad day, and even if it is a bad one, it's not as bad as it used to be. Even my shot selection changed. They've yet to invent a pill that will make you play championship snooker, but Prozac gave me the confidence to think about my game in the same way any other player might. Whereas before I'd be on 50 and thinking, Shit, I shouldn't be out of position here, this geezer's gonna think I'm crap if I can't clear the table because I should be able to, and end up playing a reckless shot, now I was happy to make a break of 50 and play a safety. I was content to think, Right, I'm 50 up, now it's your turn. You're on the back foot. If you win the frame, fair play to you, but if you make a mistake I'm going to punish you again. I'd started to think from the opponent's position rather than mine, which somehow I'd always managed to turn into doom and gloom. I was thinking objectively for the first time in four or five years. My temperament had also changed. I was no longer thinking, Let's get this session over with quickly, I just want to be out of here so I can sit in my room and watch videos and order Chinese. Now it was simply: Let's get the best out of this session, even if I lose it 5–3.

After playing Peter I went home and watched the match on the telly. The commentator John Virgo said, 'This is the best snooker I've ever seen Ronnie play. If he continues like this, he is the man to beat.' That came as a surprise to me. I was watching myself and thinking, I didn't feel that good, but I knew John Virgo was not the sort of person who would say that unless he meant it.

I was through to the semi-finals, and thought, Now the tournament really begins. I'd been to the semis three times before, but never further. Even if you don't feel you're playing too well, you realise that your match snooker must be OK to have got you so far. You've played so many frames and so many matches that you're becoming a hard player to beat.

In the semi-final I was up against Joe Swail. He'd beaten Mark Williams, which opened up the draw for me. Mark had won the World Championship the year before, and I had been expecting to play him in the semis. Joe is a quality player. You have to be half-decent even to get to Sheffield, never mind get to the semi-finals. But I was much happier playing Joe because Mark was the champion, ranked number one in the world, and he's a very tough opponent over three or four days, whereas I knew that I should beat Joe maybe eight times out of ten. Against Mark, it would have been fifty–fifty. I thought, This is a real chance to get to my first World final. In my three previous semis I'd lost to Ebdon, Higgins and Hendry, and I'd only been close in one of them, against Ebdon.

I approached it the same way I'd approached all the other matches. I didn't go to the Crucible unless I had a match to play and I didn't practise at all in Sheffield. I'd done plenty of practising that year and didn't feel I needed to do any more. Before my first-round match against Andy Hicks, Del and I were sitting in the cinema watching a film starring Pierce Brosnan at 6.30 p.m., and I was on at 7.30 p.m. It wasn't the kind of preparation that Del would have advised, but I'd told him I wanted to do it my way.

Against Joe Swail, I went 6–2 up without playing too well. I'd scored well under pressure, but it hadn't felt great. He'd make a 40 or 50 and then I'd clear up with a 70, and that hurt him. At 6–2 after the first session there was still a long way to go – it was the first to 17 frames – but I felt relaxed.

We then shared the evening session 4–4, which made the score 10–6. I was cruising, but I was beginning to feel a bit twitchy. I couldn't help thinking that I'd not been in a World final before, and how great this would be for Dad and the rest of the family. I'd had a good year, already won four tournaments, and it would be great to finish it off with getting to the final of the World.

I was speaking to Dad regularly and had told him I'd started taking the tablets. 'Great!' he said. 'I can hear the difference in your voice, and I can tell you're a lot better than you were.' He was encouraging me. 'You're looking frightening out there,' he said. 'Your aura, your presence, your long potting. Cor! You're crunching them long ones in! I was thinking he's not going for this one, is he? I'm grabbing hold of this fella's hand while you're taking a shot, thinking, Oh no, and it was in.' Dad was so excited.

In spite of the twitches, I eventually took the match 17–9. I was delighted. I came in and did an interview.

'How do you feel, Ronnie?' Everybody was interested in how I felt because of the interview I'd given on the radio at the start of the tournament when I'd said how awful I'd been feeling.

'I feel great. I'm just pleased to be in the final. I'm going to watch John Higgins and Matthew Stevens knock the stuffing out of each other tonight, and I just can't wait to play the winner. I can't believe I'm here, and I'm buzzing.' It couldn't have been more different from the first pre-tournament interview.

I went for a swim and a steam with Del. Then we went for a meal. I kept to my routine and didn't go near the practice table. In the past I'd always be obsessing about one shot or another, trying out a new grip or a new bridge, tweaking little things, looking for something to give me confidence. But I hadn't bothered with any of that in Sheffield. I just thought, If it's going to happen, it's going to happen; have a bit of faith. I felt clear-headed, and wasn't making myself miserable trying to get some new shot right. I knew that extra practice would make no difference when I'd been playing the game for sixteen years. I thought, If I don't know how to play snooker now, I never will. It's all very well having coaches telling you how to do this and that, but ultimately it has to come from within.

I'd stuck with my new philosophy right through to the final, but now I felt I had to get at least some practice in because you never get a free lunch against John Higgins – my opponent in the final. I knew it was going to be a war and I'd have to grind it out. Del agreed. I think he'd learned from the time I'd played John in the semi-finals of the World in 1998. Then he'd said to me, 'This year you're going to win the World Championship.'

I'd replied, 'What d'you mean?'

'I know it,' Del said. 'No one can beat you.'

I'd never shared that belief, and I was crucified by John, 17–9. After the match I said to Del, 'You told me I was going to win it.'

'Deep down in my heart,' he said, 'I didn't think there was any way you could lose, but there's something in your mind that's stopping you from doing it. It's not your game. It's in your head.' He pointed to my brain. 'It's them six inches. That is where you're winning and losing matches. Ron, believe me, I've seen you play for years and nobody plays the game like you, and it's in your head that you're losing these matches.'

'It's not in my head,' I said. 'My head's right if my game's right.'

'Bollocks,' he said. 'No one's game is right all the time. You've got to win matches with your head.'

Three years after we'd had that conversation we went down to the Crucible at 8 a.m. It was a 3 p.m. start, and I'd said to Del, 'We'll get down there early, have breakfast, and go for a walk along the canal.' I didn't feel too bad, but I was anxious because I thought, I've gone against the principle that I wouldn't practise. Maybe I should be at the hotel relaxing. But then I thought, Sod it, I need to play well against John Higgins. My head isn't strong enough to beat him and my bad game's not good enough to beat his bad game, because he's more consistent, more methodical than me. My mind was telling me that I needed to be inspirational to win, but I didn't mind thinking like that.

We went to do a couple of hours' practice. In a way, I wished I hadn't because I didn't feel too clever, but I went back to the hotel, relaxed, went for my little walk along the canal. At 2 p.m. I got myself ready and at two-thirty was down at the venue, where I put in fifteen minutes on the practice table. John walked in with his mate, so we were on the practice tables at the same time. I was watching him to see how he was playing, and he looked to be hitting the ball well.

Part of me was still questioning whether I deserved to be in the final. The other part was saying, Why am I questioning myself? I'm here, just enjoy it. But it's hard to enjoy the World final, and I didn't enjoy this one.

I started off well. In the first frame I let him in and he was on 30-odd and had split the pack up beautifully. Here we go, I thought, he'll polish off the frame, so just sit here patiently. But he potted a red and went off in the middle. Everybody in the crowd groaned. I hadn't expected to get back to the table that frame. I was on a long red, and I thought, If I miss this, it's a bad sign. It wasn't an easy shot, and I didn't feel comfortable on it, but I went for it with everything I had, got it, and finished on the black. I then won the frame with an 80 break.

After that, I was settled. Although I wasn't confident in my technique, the balls were going in the holes and I was making good what was there. I was playing the percentage game, not missing easy balls, playing the right shots. When there was a safety shot to play, I'd play it. At the interval I was 3–1 up.

'What d'you think?' I said to Del.

'Nice. Solid. Strong. To me, you look complete out there.'

'I don't feel it,' I said. 'I feel like shit.'

'Carry on doing what you're doing,' he said.

'D'you reckon?'

'Just keep on doing what you're doing,' he repeated. 'D'you want a cup of tea?'

'Yeah, I'd love a cup of tea.'

'Want a fag?'

'Yeah, I'd love a fag.'

'Biscuit?'

He went off and came back with the biscuits and the tea. It was like having Mum or my nan with me.

'What newspaper would you like?'

'Oh, will you get us the *Mail* and the *Sun*, Del?'

'Want a massage?'

He's so relaxing and such a laugh. No one makes me laugh like Del. He'll do anything for me. He even rubs my feet for an hour. His wife used to get a bit jealous, I think, so now he has to do her feet for an hour, too. Del is like a second father to me.

We had a talk five minutes before I went out after the interval. 'Right, concentrate. He is going to come at you. Be prepared.'

I went out there, focused, and won the next two frames. Now I was thinking about winning the World Championship. I wasn't playing too well and I was 5–1 up: only 13 frames to go. The session ended 6–2. I came out a bit disappointed, thinking I should have been 7–1 up. It's only one frame, but one frame is a two-frame swing – there's a big difference between being four frames up and six frames up.

'Listen,' said Del, 'would you have taken six–two at the start?'

'Fucking right I would have done,' I said.

'OK. Be satisfied with your afternoon's work because you've played well.'

We went back to the hotel. I told Del I didn't want anyone in my room, didn't want any phone calls. At Sheffield, I never let calls into my room: they disconnect the phone and anything I need goes up to Del's room and he'll bring it down to me. It means there's no chance of people gatecrashing on me, and me thinking I have to entertain them. In 2001 Del would come in, we'd chat, watch a video or some telly, have something to eat – a bit of chicken or salad, some carbohydrates to keep me going – and the Prozac pill at 10.30 a.m. after breakfast.

By the semi-final I'd grown used to the Prozac, so I had no worries about feeling faint or dizzy while playing. And I had a lot more energy. In the first frame of the evening session of the final I went 7–2 up, even though it was one of the worst frames of snooker I've ever played in. We both missed ball after ball after ball. I was thinking, This is embarrassing. This is the final of the World Championship, and the audience must be wondering if we're ever going to pot a ball. But that's the way it was – and you're never going to play well throughout a thirty-five-frame match. You just have to wait for it to come and play your way through the bad form. In the past I'd often lost matches because I never gave it a chance to come; I'd beaten myself up so badly that when the form did finally come it was too late, and the deficit was too great to overcome. But now my bad game wasn't so bad; I was minimising the damage I was doing.

But the poor form continued. I lost the next three frames to go in at the interval only 7–5 up.

I asked Del, 'What is going on? I'm having a nightmare. I can't pot a fucking ball.'

'Look, just stick in there,' he said. 'You're not playing badly. You've missed a few, he's missed a few. He's started to pot a few now, so just be ready for him.'

I went out there, and won three frames on the trot, with two breaks of 90 and a ton. And I felt awful through all of them: the execution just didn't feel right, and I was pissed off because the balls weren't going in the middle of the pockets. Obviously, I was being too hard on myself again.

John took the last frame of the session, but I was happy with 10–6 because at 7–5 I'd been sitting in the dressing room cursing the world, convinced I wasn't going to win.

After the session I walked back to the hotel with my mate Mickey the Mullet and Del, and I felt so relaxed it was scary. We were walking over to the BP garage to get our soft drinks for the night, and I said, 'He's such a good sportsman, that John Higgins.' And he was, because in parts of that match he must have felt like smashing his cue over his head or throwing it into the top stand. John is a great player, but in that first frame of the evening session he was missing balls that he'd normally get with his eyes closed. I was, too, but it was less of a surprise with me. John is rightly known as the most solid player in the game, and seeing him so badly out of sorts put me off. I thought I'd blown it so many times in that frame because usually you don't get second chances with John. I was putting pressure on myself because I'd built John up so high. But he kept giving me another chance. And yet he didn't show any emotion. When he missed a ball he just went back to his chair rather than playing up to the crowd as some players do when they screw up. (Mark Williams often claps himself when he does a bad shot and Stephen Hendry sometimes says, 'Thanks,' when he goes into the pack and the balls don't break kindly. The crowd think it's funny, but it's very offputting for the opponent.) John would never do that, would never suggest to the crowd that he's been incredibly unlucky or that the only reason I was at the table was because he was playing badly. I really respect him for that.

But in the final I never thought John's such a great fella that I want to lose. And the prospect of making the post-tournament speech no longer terrified me like it had that time in Scotland. That side of me had disappeared.

I came out for Sunday afternoon, and went from 10–6 to 14–7 up with breaks of 138, 90, 50 and 50. At 14–7, John was among the balls and I thought, Fair enough, I've had my little run, now it's John's turn. He missed a black off the spot, an elementary run-through, and I was out of my chair as quick as you can blink. All the balls were there for me, nothing on the cushions, and as long as I kept it tidy I'd be all right. It was a slightly tricky long-distance red, but not really a problem. I missed it. John jumped out of his chair and cleared up: 14–8. When he won the next two, I was panicking. After all, I had now overtaken Jimmy White in many people's eyes as the best player never to have won the World Championship. John had already won the World and was ranked number one at the time.

I went back to the room pissed off. Del said I should lie down and have a drink before leaving me alone. I was lying in bed when there was a knock on the door. 'What is it?' I shouted.

'It's me, Del, I've just had the doctor on the phone.'

I let him in. 'What d'you mean you've just spoken to the doctor?'

'Please, Ronnie, just phone him and have a quick chat with him.'

'What's he going to do to me?'

'He wants you to take another Prozac,' said Del. 'The doctor was watching the match on the telly, and he saw that your concentration level was falling. You were fading away.'

'What d'you mean "fading away"?' I said.

'Just talk to him, please,' said Del.

'I ain't phoning no one,' I said.

Del begged me: 'Please, Ronnie. Please.'

Finally I agreed to make the call. 'All right, Dr Hodges?'

'Hello, Ronnie,' he said.

'Look, what's the matter?' I was short with him.

'I've been watching your progress through the tournament,' he said, 'and you've been doing fantastic, but I noticed at the end of that session you were just starting to nod off a little bit. It won't affect your snooker, but it will affect your ability to stay alert. I think you need to take another tablet. Take one now, and in an hour and a half, two hours, you'll come alive again.'

This was at about 6 p.m. He was right. I did feel a bit drowsy, a bit heavy duty. So I took the tablet.

We did a bit of practice, and Del asked how I felt.

'All right, not too bad. I'm just going to go out there and try to enjoy it.' I still felt a bit tired.

The organisers said John and I were going to do the long walk tonight, from the top of the Crucible Theatre via the crowd, rather than just walking through the curtains. We got to the top, and I was feeling nervous walking there. It was the final session, make or break time. Everything is magnified enormously at the Crucible because it is the big tournament. You miss a red, and the crowd goes mental. You can't help but feel the heat of it. All of a sudden I started to feel alive. I felt awake, buzzy.

I won the first frame to go 15–10 up. Then it went 15–11, 15–12, 16–12. I might have been wide awake, but the snooker wasn't good at all. After the interval John came out and started potting balls, playing really well. He made 60 to win the frame, but then it suddenly clicked into place for me, too, and I made a 60 to win the next. At 17–13, one frame away from winning the World, I made 40 or so, played safe, and John missed to let me in. I potted a couple of reds and blacks, looked at the scoreboard, and thought, I need one more red and he's going to shake my hand. I was already thinking what I was going to say in the speech afterwards, instead of concentrating on clearing the table. I had one hand on the trophy. I missed a simple red and turned away in disgust. I looked back at the table to see what I'd left: John couldn't miss. I felt it was fate: that I was destined not to win the World. John cleared up and we were 17–14. Right at the end of the match, John was beginning to play his best snooker. He scented blood and I knew my miss had inspired him. The pressure was back on me, even though I was 17–14 up. From thinking about my victory speech I was now thinking of tomorrow's papers, with the headline HOW DID HE MANAGE TO LOSE? and all those interviews I'd have to do with people reminding me of the red I'd missed and making me explain how it had happened.

Next frame he broke. I missed a long red and before I knew it he was on 40-odd. He was looking good, then he missed a straightforward red. The boot was on the other foot now. It was me who didn't expect to be at the table, and I had to make the most of it. I ended up making the best 80 break of my life and won the World in great style. That match was as character-building for me as anything in my life. It was proof that I could win under pressure. As soon as I potted the yellow I knew I'd won the World Championship. I potted the green, brown, blue and pink, and put my cue on the table. It felt unbelievable.

John shook my hand and came out with the greatest thing he could have said: 'Tell your Dad, "Well done, I'm so pleased for you and your family." '

'You are a top man,' I said to him. 'You're a different class. Forget snooker – I don't need to tell you you're a great player. But I've got so much respect for you as a man. You're a gentleman, one hundred per cent.'

We've always got on because we're similar people. John's family are very close, and we're very close. We come from similar backgrounds, and we know our family is more important than managers and the press.

When I won, the first thing I thought was, Where's Mum? She's got to be around somewhere. I saw her being held up by my girlfriend at the time, Bianca. Mum came running up to me, tears in her eyes, and she was bouncing around like she couldn't believe it.

This was all I'd dreamed of. I just wanted to pick up the trophy, and for once I wanted to kiss it. I thought, I want to press my lips right on that. My sister Danielle had come up with her boyfriend, but she'd missed me winning it. She caught me picking up the trophy, though, and she started crying as well. We'd not always been so close, but in the past couple of years we've come together much more.

'What are you crying for?' I said.

'I'm so proud of you. I'm so happy. You've done brilliant.'

'Come here, and give me a cuddle,' I said. 'Come

on! It's good to cry. We're all happy. Come in the dressing room. I want you in there.'

There was me, Mum, Danielle, Del, Jimmy White, Ronnie Wood and Ronnie Wood's wife Jo all crammed in this tiny dressing room and everyone was lifting the trophy above their head, and going mad. I was the calmest person there.

Jimmy had come back from his holiday for the final and I was so chuffed to see him there. At the same time I felt so disappointed for him, seeing someone he was close to winning the World. It had meant so much to him and he had been desperate to win it, but he'd lost in six finals. I felt like giving him the trophy and saying, 'Here, you have it for a year.' If there is one thing I could wish for him, it's a World Championship, and to be there to shake his hand and have a good night with him afterwards. I know what it would do for him because I know what it's done for me. It's buried so many demons. If I'd finished my career and never won it, there would have always been a little cloud over me – was I really good enough? Despite everything I've won, I would always have thought I'd not had the bottle or the will to win the big one. And it does take a lot of bottle, as well as luck, to win it.

Del's grin was so big it split his face in two. He gave me a massive cuddle and a kiss on the cheek. 'Well done!' he said. 'Enjoy it! I love ya.'

'I love ya, too,' I said.

We went back stage and all of a sudden Del, who is normally so calming, became panicky – 'We've got to do the press, we've got to do this, we've got to do that.' He gets nervous when it's right to get nervous. I'm not a great one for doing the TV and the papers, but Del said, 'It's good for you, and only fair to the fans who have paid the money.' My instinct was to go right back to the hotel, have a few drinks and really start the party, but Del put on his sensible hat and made sure we did all we had to do.

There was one niggling thought – the dinner. Then again, I thought, I'm so happy, I could just go up there and say, 'Thank you,' and that would say it all. Nothing else needed to be said. We went back to the hotel and I didn't even bother to get changed. John Higgins was in a smart suit and tie, and I was still in my waistcoat. The last thing I wanted to do was get changed. I just wanted to lap it up. I could have flown that night if I'd had wings.

John gave a really funny speech. 'When we were juniors,' he said, 'everybody was talking about Ronnie O'Sullivan. I was in Scotland and he was in England, and I just wanted to see what he looked like and how he played. When I finally saw him, I couldn't believe he was only fourteen – he had a big beard, was about five foot ten, and was knocking in hundred breaks. I looked him up and down and thought, There is no way he's fourteen – twenty-eight more like.'

Everybody started laughing, and it reminded me of my first memories of John when he beat me in Prestatyn. About a month after that he won the biggest junior competition there was – the World Sky

Meter Masters, beating me on the way. Then Ian Doyle signed him up. That was it – we were rivals. I was with Barry Hearn, who was English, and John was with Ian Doyle, who was Scottish. Barry had Steve Davis in his stable; Ian had Stephen Hendry. They were the fiercest rivals. Now they were pitting me against John, and people were asking which of us was going to be World Champion first. In the end, it was John, closely followed by me.

When I went up to make my speech I was introduced with: 'And here we have the 2001 World Champion ...' Everybody was clapping and cheering. I felt great making the speech, relaxed. I hadn't had a drink all night, and the words just poured out spontaneously. After saying how much I admired John as a player and a man, I thanked everyone and told them I was off to have a good night of it.

After the speeches, I went to the bar with Mum, Danielle, John and his family. By about 2 a.m. John was pissed out of his head and I was getting there. Mum was already gone. The dad of John's girlfriend, Denise, has got a bald head, and Mum was slapping it all night. When she gets drunk she gets a bit carried away, and she can say anything. She was saying to him, 'Oh, you've got a lovely head, you have, let me kiss it,' and she was kissing and slapping his head. He was loving it, sitting there with a big grin on his face. We were all laughing. It was such a great night.

At about six in the morning, I said, 'I've got to go to bed, I'm knackered.' I walked back with Mum, Del and John Higgins's mum. My mum and John's mum were singing all sorts of songs. We got to the end of the road and John's mum said, 'Well done, I'm pleased for you. Although I would have liked to have seen my John win, the next person I wanted to see win was you. I'm over the moon for you.'

The first time I spoke to Dad after winning the World was later that day. I'd just got home at 6 p.m., having driven all the way back from Sheffield. I cooked everyone pasta – I was in my cooking mode then – and the phone rang. Mum answered. It was Dad.

'I can't believe it,' he said, 'I'm walking around here ten feet tall. It's unreal. I've been up from midnight till eight in the morning just listening to the news every hour: "New World Champion Ronnie O'Sullivan". How did you do it? You played marvellous. I'm so happy, I can't want for no more.'

'I'm coming up to see you next week, Dad,' I said.

Even though he was in prison, it felt like we'd done it together – that we were still a team. I thought back to all the years he'd come to watch me practise down at the club, and how he moved house just so he could have a snooker room built for me. The partnership was split up when he went away, and I never knew whether I would have the self-belief to make a success of myself without him there to support me. At last I'd proved I did have.

It hadn't sunk in that I'd won. We were so excited, but all I wanted to do was sit down and be with the people I'd been with for the whole two and a half weeks: Del, my Scouse mates John and Ronnie, and

Mickey the Mullet. If I'd had my way, I would have sat in a room with them for a few hours and just buzzed over what we'd done. It was only a few days later when we could do that. We were all still buzzing reliving the tournament, the Chinese meals delivered to the room, Del's panics, my depression, my pills, the feeling that this could be our year despite everything, the whole range of emotions.

Two weeks later, at the next tournament, the Matchroom League in Inverness, I had time to reflect properly with Del and Mickey the Mullet. It was the first time I'd arrived at a tournament, got to the hotel, and been put in the suite. There were twenty-nine floors and I was on the twenty-eighth. Nobody could get up to the floor unless they had the key.

'They must have put everyone up here,' I said to Del.

'No, I'm on the nineteenth floor,' he said.

I called him from my room. 'Oi, Del, come and look at my room,' I said. It had tellies and fridges and big rocking chairs. 'What's all this about?'

'That's what you get for being World Champion,' he said.

'You're joking!'

But he was right. Every tournament I've been to since then, they've given me a suite in the hotel. It's so strange that the more successful you become, the more people want to give you things. And the more you can afford, the more people want to give you things for nothing. It doesn't seem right.

Even though the Matchroom League isn't a

massive tournament, I just wanted to be playing, because I'd started looking forward to my snooker. I had to play John Higgins in the semis, and I beat him 6–3. Neither of us played that well, but my belief carried me through. I was still struggling quite badly with my technique, compared to when I was 14, 15 or 16, but I was playing with experience and confidence.

I beat Stephen Hendry 9–7 in the final. He had a bit of bad luck in that match. He should have gone 8–5 up, but I made it 7–6, and then won two of the last three frames. Winning was now becoming a habit. I expected to win, even if I wasn't in the best form.

The press, unsurprisingly, were wondering if I felt any different about the game and myself.

'To be honest,' I said, 'I just want to enjoy the moment. I can't believe I've won the World title. I want to have the summer off, and relax and enjoy it.' At the time I was into my recovery, so I was looking for a spiritual way of living. 'I just want to live for the moment. Tomorrow's not important, next month is not important, what's happened in the past is not important. That is my journey. And I don't know what will happen in three or four months, I don't know if I will play next season, but this is a great feeling and what I've worked all my life for.'

The press were good to me. I've had a fair few run-ins with them, but I think most were pleased for me. They have written bad pieces about me, but generally they've been deserved. They hurt at the time, but they were just what I needed – articles saying, 'Ronnie, get your finger out.' After I'd done the interviews, Tex Hennessy, who had taken me out for dinner with his wife all those years ago and had also given me a hammering when I'd needed it, came up to me and said, 'You don't realise how happy you've made me. You've made my day and my year.' It was lovely.

That season I won the World, I won three tournaments before Christmas, reached the final of another, and got to the semis of a fifth. It was a phenomenal run for me. Then I didn't win anything for three or four tournaments, but came back to win the Irish Masters, the World and the Matchroom League. So all in all, that season I won six out of the twelve tournaments I contested. It was the second most successful season for a snooker player (Stephen Hendry once won seven tournaments in a season). I was so proud of that.

What made me particularly proud was that I knew I was playing snooker in an era when the competition has never been so great and the standard so high. It means more now to win the World Championship than when Steve Davis won all of his titles. He'd probably trade in three of the six he's won to win one today, because to win today you'd have to beat the likes of Hendry, White, Higgins, Ebdon, Doherty and me to get there. The Nugget was and still is my hero, but in his day he could lift the World by beating Doug Mountjoy in the final. It was a different era.

When the Nugget won his last Bensons in 1997 he beat Hendry in the quarters, Ken Doherty in the semis, and me in the final, and I know just how much it meant to him. He'd rolled back the years, and you could see he was a class act and could compete with the younger generation.

My second-best season was in 1997 when I won four tournaments and got to the final of a couple of others. I won the Thailand Masters, the German Open, the Irish Benson and Hedges and the Matchroom League: none of them massive events. To win six titles, including the World, was dreamland for me. It's still sinking in two seasons on.

Every morning after I won it I'd get up and the trophy would be there. I'd look at it and think, I can't believe that's in my front room. In the next season I won the UK, so I had the World and the UK – snooker's two biggest trophies – sitting next to each other in Mum's living room. That gave me such a buzz.

I won one other tournament in 2001-2, and got to a couple of finals. It doesn't compare with the previous season, but I know I should be happy with that. If you win one of the big tournaments in a season, you're doing well. Even Stephen Hendry and Steve Davis, at their peaks, have gone eighteen months without winning a tournament. What pleased me in that season when I was World Champion was my general consistency. Even when I wasn't winning tournaments, I was getting through to the quarters and semis, so I was always knocking on the door, just a fag paper away from winning four or five tournaments. The funny thing was that I felt my game was better in that year than in the year before, when I had won the six tournaments. Perhaps the main difference is that I feel I know how I'm going to play when I go out for a match.

Defending the World Championship was tough. Everybody kept telling me that no first-time winner had won the following season. But I did feel I could do it. I wanted it, but I knew I didn't want it as much as I had the year before; I didn't want it enough. It was only in the month after I'd lost to Hendry in the semi-final that I realised how gutted I was that I hadn't won the World for a second time.

The consolation was that I was number one in the world for the first time, but I wanted the World Championship and World Number One at the same time. The ranking system is based on two years, so I had the year when I won six tournaments and 2001–2 when I won two both counting. It felt great, but I couldn't be totally satisfied without the World title. I have to learn from that, so when I'm in the same position again I don't become complacent and think, It's OK to get beat here, I can relax because I've done enough this year and got to number one.

That's not to say I didn't want to beat Stephen Hendry badly in that semi-final. I made it perfectly clear on television just how badly I wanted to beat him. But in the end, probably partly because of what I'd said, he wanted it more than me. I contributed to my own downfall. It was a silly thing to say because it fired and inspired him, and I put myself up there to be shot down. And he duly shot me down. If I'd had my time over again, I wouldn't have said it. Perhaps I'd have two World Championships by now if I'd kept shtum.

CHAPTER TWELVE

The Future

It seems so long ago that I was desperate to give up the game and couldn't see any future for myself. As I write this I've never felt so calm, optimistic and together. I hope I'm still feeling the same when you read it.

It's been due to a mixture of things – Prozac, the Priory, going to meetings, not abusing my body on a regular basis, learning about myself by doing the Twelve Steps, winning the World Championship, and my girlfriend Jo.

I have slipped off the wagon a few times. Jumped off, actually. Those were the times when I thought I had it all sussed, had beaten my addictions, and wanted to go out and enjoy myself because I thought I was missing out. But I can't live with it any more. It never sat right with me when I first started puffing and drinking, and it still doesn't sit right with me today.

I've found what makes me truly happy: being straight with myself and starting to understand what I'm about as a person. I really want to know my weaknesses, and feel that I can now cope with that knowledge. Maybe I am spoiled, selfish, arrogant. I can't say it's always been this way, but I feel that I am quite a humble person today. I also feel I don't have to strut around proving myself to others. I was always useless at it anyway.

Prozac worked like a miracle. It took away my fears and anxieties. I don't care if I have to stay on it for the rest of my life. I'm not ashamed of taking Prozac. It makes me feel well, and it enables me to get on with my life. If you are a depressive the first thing to do is admit it and then do something about it. Now I can get up in the morning and look forward to whatever is put in front of me. Life's a challenge and my snooker's a challenge, and for a long time neither was.

I've changed as a person: I want to enjoy life, spend quality time with friends and family, and talk about things much more than I used to. I've had enough bad years of depression and doing things for other people, trying to keep everyone happy. People never said it, but there was always a feeling in the family that if I was doing well everyone was happy. But that's bollocks. It's much more about being happy inside. And for so long none of us ever told each other how we felt deep down. I'd tell Mum and Dad that I was miserable, but never really talked about why. Now Dad can tell from the tone of my voice whether I'm happy or not. He's had enough years of hearing me depressed, and now I get a buzz out of him ringing up and asking if I'm OK, and I can tell him yes. I love talking to him openly about everything that's happened in the day. Beforehand, I was in such a bad state that he was always trying to jack me up – which was crazy with me travelling the world playing snooker and him in prison.

Every year I'd think about packing in the game, then I'd have my three-month break in the summer and I'd be all geared up, refreshed, the brain decharged, and I'd think I could handle another season of snooker. But after a week of it I'd be on the phone moaning to Dad again, and we'd go through the same old routine: 'OK, get this season out of the way,' he'd say, 'and then you can put your cue down.' For six or seven years the conversation went on like this. I just used to moan and he was there to help me. I'd forget all that he was going through. I was so selfish, so self-absorbed that I wasn't well. It must have been torture for him listening to me, but he was so strong that he put his own troubles aside to make sure I was all right.

In all that time, I never really examined myself. But by going into the Priory and getting to know myself I now won't just scratch the surface. When I feel strongly I have to tell people.

Winning that first tournament, the Champions Cup, after my stay in the Priory was in many ways my greatest achievement. It was so special for me and I was full of optimism. I thought, Yes, I've got my life back. I made a speech and said, 'It's lovely to be here, but you're going to see a different Ronnie; you've seen a bit of a nutty one up till now, but I can assure you that there will be a lot of changes.' And I think there have been.

Dad and I talk and laugh these days.

He recently said to me, 'When you get to forty your life will be the best.'

'How can you say that?' I said. 'You was banged up when you was forty.'

'I know,' he said. 'But when you get to forty life begins.'

I thought, You're having a laugh. How can he come out with a statement like that when he's spent the past twelve years inside? But it just shows the strength of him. It's a strength that's surprised even him. He always said he could never handle prison, that he couldn't do a day in the nick. But on visits mates of his on the inside have told me, 'Your dad is a one-off. He has done his prison like no one else I know. He's so strong.' Although he gives the appearance that nothing could affect him, and laughs things off, that is his way of dealing with prison. But I know deep down he desperately wants to come home; and he does have a lot of remorse.

These days, more than ever, Dad says I shouldn't do anything I don't want to do. He often tells me that I have more than exceeded any hopes or expectations he had of me. 'I wanted you to turn professional, that was my dream,' he said recently. 'You turned professional, and then I thought, If you get in the top thirty-two, or get on the telly ... and you did that. Then I thought, Well, maybe if you win a tournament ... and you did that. Then I thought, If you won the World title, I would do another ten years in here ... and you did that. If someone told me you'd be number one, I would have got out the baby oil and I would have just lay there. Every time I've set my goal and said, "I hope my boy can do that," every time you've exceeded it. So I couldn't care less if you potted another ball or not. Go and enjoy it now. You've fulfilled everything I ever dreamed for you, and you've done everything I ever dreamed of doing. I wanted to be a footballer, but I was never quite good enough. I wasn't good enough, but you are. And in years to come, they will ask where it all started, and they'll say a little East End fella with the porno shops had a boy who was a snooker player ... And then I want you to have a boy who can follow on from you and maybe become a Formula One driver, and I'll be happy with it starting at me.'

Del always said to me, 'Buy a raffle ticket and you've got a chance. Just buy the raffle ticket and give yourself the chance of winning it.' Now it feels like I've got the raffle ticket when I'm playing. Before, I thought, If the opponent plays well, I'm in trouble. Now I think, If I play well, they're in trouble, and even if I don't play well, I've still got half a chance of winning. Now I don't go into a match thinking I've got to be at my best throughout. I know that hardly ever happens. If I go 3–1 down, I think, Well, he's had his good session, now it's my turn. It's been hard to train myself into that way of thinking, but I've done it.

They say that your strengths are also your weaknesses, and it's certainly true in my case. I'm a perfectionist, and it has caused me so much pain – obsessing about not being able to do things as well as I want to. But on balance I'm glad I'm a perfectionist because if I wasn't I probably would have thrown in the towel a long time ago. I have to look at it as an asset, but I need to let it go sometimes, otherwise it will drag me down. It's OK to be a perfectionist, as long as you don't make yourself ill over it, which is what I did for all those years.

Trophies are great, but I still get more pleasure from just playing well. I get a bigger buzz from playing well down the club than from playing badly and winning in a competitive match. Having total control over the cue ball is as exciting for me now as it was when I was a kid. It was losing that buzz that made me want to give up the game. But I stuck in there with the help of Mum and Dad, and eventually got it back. At some points I definitely felt that I would have rather worked for Dad's business. Maybe I would have been happy selling books and videos, and having people come in and say, 'Did you used to be Ronnie O'Sullivan, the snooker player?' There were times when I would have settled for that just to lead a balanced, happy life. I ran the conversations through my head. People would come in the shop, see me, and then ask what had happened. 'Oh, you know, I got hacked off with the game. I couldn't handle it, so I just decided not to play.' I was certain at those times that the only way I'd ever be happy again was by quitting snooker, but I still had memories of myself as a little kid, down the club at nine in the morning, brushing the baize, then on the table all day. That kid loved his snooker so much, and I couldn't get that memory out of my head either.

I know I'll have good and bad days. The difference now is that I accept that. I think I'm seeing things more objectively, and playing more consistently as a result. I've also worked on my technique. Since coming out of the Priory I've had extra support from a coach called Frank Adamson, the coach of Stephen Lee. Frank has helped me out so much with my game. Without him, I don't think I would have won the World Championship and I certainly wouldn't have won six tournaments in that season. Frank, who is 74, analysed my game and told me I was rushing shots. We looked at videos of when I was younger and everything seemed more deliberate and leisurely. As I got older I didn't seem to be chalking the cue properly, and I wasn't setting myself up correctly for the shot, just taking it for granted and falling into it. By playing so quickly people had the impression that I thought I couldn't miss a pot. But the reason for the speed couldn't have been more different. I played so quickly because I *lacked* confidence. While lots of players who are having problems would go slower and slower, my way of dealing with it was to go faster and faster. I just thought, I'm not going to think about it. My natural game is potting and instinct, and that's what beats opponents. I told myself that my unpredictability was my strength, but I think I was underestimating myself. Today, I hope, I've recovered some of the calmness and consistency of my game as a 15-year-old. Before Frank the balls went in at 100 m.p.h. or they didn't go in at all. Now they seem to go in on a much more regular basis.

We looked at so many other things, too. Was it my stance, was it my shoulders, was I holding the cue too tight, was I too near the ball, was I too far from the ball, was I setting up too much on the left-hand side of the ball, was I setting up too much on the right-hand side of the ball, was I coming underneath the shot, was my left foot too far forward, too far back? I didn't know where the root of the problem was, so we deconstructed my game and examined everything. I still don't know what it is today, and I still have the problem, but it's not as bad as it was. I can hit through a ball, I'm sighting the ball better, although still not as well as I'd like to, and I know that on my day I'm capable of winning tournaments. When I was at my lowest I'd lost that belief. I felt I had to rely on others not to play so well for me to win, and that pissed me off. I thought, Why play the game if you're relying on another opponent not to play well? And if he did play well, I thought my technique would let me down. Now, with the help of Frank and Del, some of the basic things I wasn't doing are natural in my game. I know not to feather so fast, to have a bit of a pause, to cue straight and go through the ball nice and slowly. Frank showed me two or three vital things, but the rest I've added in for myself. As I said to him, 'You may want me to play in a certain way, but I still have to put my own bits in, whether it's having my cue higher off the table, whether it's putting more weight on my left leg, I still have to add those little bits because they're what make me as a player.' And, however brilliant a coach Frank is, I would never want to be without Del, because he brings me coaching *and* inspiration. I need Del at tournaments because we can have a laugh: he's more my age, I feel comfortable around him, and we're a team.

Something that is important to the whole family is appealing against Dad's sentence. I think his sentence has been incredibly harsh, and it's something we are fighting to get reduced. Dad has been a rock for me, and now it's time to do something for him. As I've said, it was terrible that a man got killed, but we have always considered it to be an act of self-defence. Perhaps it's too late to appeal against the original conviction, but it's certainly not too late to appeal against the length of sentence. Why did he get eighteen years? We were told that it was because it was a racist attack, but we know that a) it wasn't a racist attack and b) he's not a racist. He's not saying he wasn't involved in the fight. He was, and he made a big mistake in acting on the advice he got to insist on his right to silence and not tell his side of the story. Dad was terrified – terrified of what he'd done, and terrified of going to prison. And he certainly made a mistake in not talking, not explaining everything that had happened to the judge and jury in court. But that's the past, and there's no undoing that. What can be done, though, is to make people understand that in spite of the judge's misguided comment, Dad isn't a racist.

Since Dad has been away the strength of the whole family – Danielle, Mum, Dad himself, even me, in my own way – has astonished me. Perhaps Mum has been most amazing of all. When I think back to the time that Dad went away and people told her that she would never be able to keep the business together, and what she has made of herself now, I feel so proud of her.

My sister Danielle is 20 and lives with her boyfriend. We are much closer now than we were when we were growing up. It was very hard for Danielle when Dad went away. She was only 9 at the time, but I think she handled it brilliantly – far better than I did. At times, both of us have felt that the other was favoured by Mum and Dad, but in our hearts we know it's rubbish, and that they love us equally.

I hope that I'll be able to get closer to my daughter Taylor soon, too. There have been problems between me and her mum, but we're starting to sort them out so that I can see much more of Taylor. Family's the most important thing in life for me, and she's definitely a part of that.

I recently opened a shop in Old Compton Street in Soho. It's called Viva La Diva and sells classy exotic underwear for men and women. I bought it as a freehold, an investment. It's the thirteenth property

I've bought since I started playing snooker professionally. It's been great for me because the housing market has gone through the roof in that time.

When I bought my first property, I was so insecure about my snooker, and I thought, I'll get sussed out on the table so I'd better invest some of the money to have something to fall back on. My manager at the time, Ian Doyle, suggested that I invest in property.

'No, I need something day to day,' I said. 'I buy property and then what? I still have to go and play snooker.'

'Just do yourself a favour and buy a few properties, and you can't go wrong,' he said.

It was great advice, the best thing Ian ever did for me. I've enjoyed having the properties, turning them into shops, meeting new people. It's been an education. Now I'm halfway through my snooker career I've got an interest away from the game. I always felt there was a bit of a businessman in me; always looking to see if there was an angle in something – even back in the days when I traded football cards at junior school. At first I bought a few houses and flats, and then moved on to commercial properties. I'd buy the freehold and give the shop to Mum for nothing. Then we started up a few more shops, which gave Mum a good income, while I kept the freehold. So everyone was happy.

The shop in Old Compton Street is in a great location – right in the heart of Soho and rather posh – and it's a boutique on two floors. The Prince of

Denmark, a designer, has done some stuff for us, and my girlfriend Jo has got a good eye for clothes, so she runs the shop. We're hoping to expand Viva La Diva and open up branches in Newcastle, Manchester, Glasgow, Edinburgh and Birmingham, but for the while I'll be happy to make a success of this one. When I give up snooker I'll take over the businesses. At the moment, thankfully, that seems a long way away, but it's nice to have something to look forward to.

I've also just set up a management firm with Jim McKenzie, who was the chief executive of the World Snooker Association. It's called Rocket Promotions. We're going to buy a few snooker clubs, find some young talent and give them proper management. We'd like to have five or six snooker halls up and down the country – places for kids who want to succeed. If we concentrate on sponsorship deals and accounts and booking their hotels, the kids can then concentrate on their snooker. Maybe they wouldn't want the full management deal and would just want us to book hotels for them or help them out with their game; so be it, we want to do what the player feels comfortable with. Too often in snooker young players are presented with no choice and have no say in their future. We want to change all that.

I'd like to keep involved in snooker in another way when I've finished playing – doing a bit of commentating and telly presenting. I see Steve Davis now and he looks more happy and relaxed than ever.

There are so many doors that can be opened, and

for the first time I can see them opening, rather than shutting in my face. I've learned to be content, and snooker is a massive part of that, but if somebody told me tomorrow that I'd never be able to play again, I know now that there's so much more to life than being a snooker player.

At the moment I'm playing golf and I'm not satisfied with being able to hit a good shot. I want to go round in level par. I've now set a goal that when I'm 50 I want to be on the Seniors' Tour playing professional golf. And I think, Why shouldn't I be, now that I've got this new optimism? Now I believe anything is possible if you put your mind to it.

Actually, I've got an even more ambitious goal than that: I want to be playing professional within five years. I don't intend to give up the snooker, but I am good enough to compete on the golf circuit. I'm not daft enough to think I could play at the level I've played snooker, but I can play well enough to give me pleasure and a sense of achievement.

At the same time, while I think it's great that I feel so optimistic, I also need to give myself regular reality checks – first things first, don't project too far ahead, live for today, and get through today before you start planning the future. That's what the Priory was about – preparing us to live in the world realistically, in the present.

It's not that I feel good all the time. Far from it. I woke up this morning and felt terrible. The panic attack was on me. But I took one of my tablets and within ten minutes I was feeling OK. How simple is that? I knew that despite how I felt when I woke up, I could go out and enjoy my day. The panic attacks only come on now when I've not taken the tablets for two or three days, which means that when I take them, I know I can relax.

Last night at the snooker club I saw a girl I'd not seen for years – Tina.

'You seem so much more content, so much happier,' she said. 'Are you happy?'

'Yes, I am,' I told her.

'It's so good to see,' she said, 'because before you were like spoiled Ronnie – the boy with all the talent. I remember you being like: "I've got all this ability. Why am I not winning? I'm not happy." You were quite arrogant,' she said.

'Was I really?'

'Yes, you were, and you've changed so much. You're a nice fella now,' she said.

That meant so much to me. Because for so long, every time I walked into a room, I used to put the mockers on it; I could bring an atmosphere down instantly if things weren't right. That used to make me feel so bad about myself. Now I walk into a room, 'Hello, how are you? Nice to meet you,' and it feels good, and I feel good about myself. I can be in people's company without thinking that I'm not good enough to be there, or thinking that I can't speak my mind. Now I feel that I can speak my mind without being horrible and offending people. I think I'm easier on myself and that makes me easier on other people.

I had always blamed my depression on snooker. I thought that every time I played well I wasn't so depressed, and every time I played badly I was more depressed. So I made the simple deduction that it was just the game that brought me down. But I had an illness and didn't realise it. After I started taking Prozac I discovered that I could play badly, be upset that I played badly, but still be happy as a person. To me, that is progress. Massive progress.

I always look back nostalgically to the time when I was 14, 15 and 16 and I was just turning professional. I think that's when my snooker was at its best, and when I was happiest in life. I'm sure now that I was playing so well because I felt happy and balanced, rather than the other way round. That period in my life has always been my golden age, the time I've wanted to recapture – on and off the table. I know I've done a lot of damage to myself over the years, but I feel I'm beginning to get back there.

EPILOGUE

It's a year now since I wrote the book, and it's been a pretty topsy-turvy time. There's been three tournaments won, far too many first-round defeats, a record-breaking, televised 147 at the World Championship, closely followed by first-round defeat by Marco Fu, the odd relapse, and very strange (but not wholly unfounded) stories on the front pages of the newspapers about me becoming a Muslim.

Snooker-wise, the season started off really well. I won the first tournament, the Regal Scottish Masters, in September 2002, and then it got progressively worse until it got better again. I was feeling so positive, fit and optimistic at the beginning of the season. In Scotland, I played well against Stephen Hendry in the semis and managed to beat him 6–3, and played well against John Higgins, who I beat 9–4 in the final. One tournament down, one trophy won. My game seemed to be coming together, and I was really enjoying it – much more so than when I won the World Championship when I was just doing it rather than enjoying it. I wasn't flying like when I was a kid, but I was buzzing in the right direction.

Then things went from bad to worse. I played

terribly in the UK championship in York. I was so disappointed because that was one I particularly wanted to win. I won my first-round match 9–2, but thought it was some of the worst snooker I'd ever played (you've heard that from me before, haven't you?) and then I beat Marco Fu 9–7 – again after an awful spell in the first session. In the quarters I was drawn against Drew Henry, and everyone expected me to win. But I played really poorly. I was so uninvolved in the game I didn't feel I was there. I defy anybody to enjoy something when they are playing as badly as I was.

I ended up watching the game on the next table more than I was watching my own game. I kept leaning my head round because Ken Doherty was playing John Higgins and it was a much more interesting game than mine; I heard the crowd clapping at the big breaks and felt I was missing out on something. Drew Henry ended up beating me 9–6. When I was 4–2 down, I was playing so badly that I reverted back to the left-handed business, which made me interested again. I won the last two frames left-handed and went into the final session 4–4. But in the evening session I went back to playing right-handed, and with hindsight perhaps I should have kept playing left-handed because I was actually enjoying it more.

Steve Davis was commentating on the telly and he said that you can tell when Ronnie's not happy with his game because he starts playing left-handed. That's a fair comment – some commentators have suggested that I do it to take the piss out of who I'm playing, but that is so far removed from the truth. In fact, I do it when I'm pissed off with myself. So perhaps when players see me using my left hand they should get a boost and realise they are in the driving seat. This season I'd like to shake things up a bit by using my left hand when I'm playing well, so it would become harder for other players to work out my state of mind.

I seemed to lose virtually every match mid-season. But then in the last third of the season suddenly things came good. In March 2003 I won the European Open, and then straight after, I won the Irish Masters. I was settting up a property company with a woman who was into positive thinking, and she asked me if I'd consider going to see a sports psychologist because I'd told her that snooker was driving me nuts again. She got a list of sports psychologists from the former footballer Alan Brazil, and we checked them all out before I decided to visit someone called Pete Cohen.

I was very sceptical, convinced that no one would be able to get me out of the doldrums. But I told myself to keep an open mind; you never know, this could be the answer, however unlikely. I went to his house in Brighton, and he started doing motivational techniques with me, trying to get me wanting to play the game again. There were times when I didn't actually want to pick up a cue because it was so frustrating for me. His job was to get me enjoying the game again, and he said once the enjoyment came the hunger would return and once the hunger returned the form would come.

At one stage, he was trying to get me to believe in myself more. He asked me who my sporting heroes were. I mentioned Muhammad Ali, Tiger Woods, Carl Lewis and Michael Johnson. So he got pictures of all of them, and had a photo of me in the middle, surrounded by greatness. He told me I was one of them, and that I had to put the pictures up in my bedroom in front of my bed to inspire me, and constantly remind me of my 'greatness'.

I tried to be open-minded about it, but deep down, whatever problems I have I do have belief in myself and don't feel I need to be told that I'm great. I know I can play the game, I have faith in my ability, but I know I don't make the most of that ability often enough, and for me that is frustrating. It's like having a powerful gun that isn't loaded. All I want is for my game to be good for 60–70 per cent of the time, and I don't mind if it's non-existent for the rest. But sometimes it's non-existent for 70 per cent of the time, and that's just not good enough. I'm not in search of perfection, just consistency. And consistency isn't something unrealistic for me to look for, especially when you consider the number of consecutive victories I had in Blackpool when I first turned professional. Consistency was one of my trademarks then.

Somewhere along the line I've lost that consistency, and I think it's partly because I've got technical about the game. There are times when I've got in my own way, and stopped trusting what I do naturally. What's most frustrating is that I remember so clearly the days when I just used to get down, no worries, and pot balls for fun. Actually, it's not the remembering that's frustrating, it's the fact that I've been unable to repeat it in recent years.

Pete and I would talk before and after tournaments. He was interested in working with someone like me, someone willing to try anything. He could see that I was very intense about my work, and if I said I'd give something a try I would do. We both got a lot out of it. Every two weeks I'd go down to his place in Brighton and play golf. We did all sorts of stuff, things that would have seemed ridiculous if I'd done them in front of anybody else, but I didn't feel inhibited in front of him. We did a lot of visualisation and sound-effects stuff to clear the mind. In a way, what we were doing was a form of meditation based on Buddhist teachings. It's all about the mind being still and being focused on yourself. When I'm playing well my focus is OK, but when I'm struggling I lose my focus. But of course, it's a bit of a chicken-and-egg situation: perhaps I'm not playing well because I'm not focused, rather than the other way round. I certainly know I couldn't stay focused against Drew Henry, and feel I did pretty well to stay as focused as I did against Marco Fu in last year's World Championship. I felt so awful in that game that I just didn't want to be there.

People assume that at least I must have been feeling great when I made the 147, but believe me I wasn't.

I felt dreadful, and couldn't believe all the balls were going in the holes. It was a perfect 147, not a fluke among the balls, but I felt awful throughout. The only consolation, and fair enough it was some consolation, was that I hadn't gone to Sheffield, got rumped in the first round and walked away with ten grand in my pocket. At least I walked away with £200,000, which meant that even though I was knocked out in the first round I was the second-biggest money earner at Sheffield.

But if I had the choice I would much rather have swapped the 147 for a win. Next day when I was sitting by myself and reflecting on it, I realised just how disappointed I was with myself, but there was nothing I could do about it. You've just got to be philosophical and wait another twelve months to try again. But the money from the 147 did soften the blow. Great, I thought, at least that gives me enough to buy a couple of new properties; so the money was an enabler. But that's all. I was gutted, really, and I responded in the worst possible way. I went back on to the drink.

I'd actually started drinking again after winning the tournament in Ireland. From there, I went to Manchester, stayed with some mates and ended up getting drunk every night. I knew I had the World Championship coming up, and realised exactly how important that was to me, but I couldn't control myself. Vodka, Southern Comfort and lemonade, beers – essentially I was living out of a suitcase. I'd won two tournaments back-to-back, and being an idiot I thought to myself, well, I can't really improve on that, and fell into the trap of thinking I was cured of my addictions. Pete Cohen had started to help me to think positively – a bit too positively, really. I stopped thinking of myself as an addict. He told me I'd got my life under control and if I fancied a drink I should have one, and being impressionable I took that on board.

It set off the whole process of denial again. I'm not an alcoholic, so I don't need to worry if I have the occasional drink. But I've never been able just to have a couple of beers, and it was stupid to think anything had changed. I soon discovered it hadn't: after a couple of beers I wanted a couple more, then a couple more, and on it went until I was slaughtered.

I was having ten-hour binges, going through from five in the evening till two and three in the morning then getting up first thing and running it off, then starting again early evening. I'd go into the gym for half an hour and think, If I drink, well, at least I can train and get it out of my system. If I got myself in decent condition at least I wouldn't turn up at Sheffield looking as if I'd come in off the streets.

So I gave myself a week of total abstinence before Sheffield to get my head together. It was such a crazy short-term approach. While in retrospect I didn't agree with everything Pete had told me – certainly not that I was fit to drink in moderation – a lot of what he had said had had a positive effect on me, but I just wasted it. Instead of going back to Chigwell after winning the two tournaments on the trot, the first thing I thought was, Great, I'm back playing well, I'll go and celebrate with the people who know how to celebrate in my way. And the next day instead of getting serious about what I had to do, I'd just be depressed.

I'm not saying that's why I got beat at Sheffield, but it can't have helped. And it continued after the World Championship. As soon as tournaments are over for me, I can't bear to watch them on the telly. There's nothing worse than the snooker being on after you've been knocked out and everyone is talking about it. I stayed at Sheffield for about three days. I'd go to the Crucible and have a couple of drinks, then I'd disappear into nearby bars or invite all my friends back to the hotel. At least I had sufficient restraint not to get totally hammered in front of all the other players.

Actually, I just wanted to get away from them. I don't feel comfortable with most of the players at the best of times. I just go into the snooker environment to do my work, and once I'm focused I can handle it, but I wouldn't be going to snooker tournaments just to say hello to the people there because I don't have a lot in common with most of them.

After staying around Sheffield, I had a few days back in London, and a few days in Manchester. Then it all came to a head. I was drinking again, and went on a six-week bender. Soon enough I was really depressed again and thought to myself, I can't go on like this. And that's when I decided I needed to go back to the rooms, Narcotics Anonymous, and sort my life out.

All the time I'd been wrecking myself, I'd kept well clear of the rooms. I would have been ashamed to have turned up in that state. And for the first few weeks I didn't think I needed to anyway: I was in control of my drinking, and just having a good time. Pete told me I was strong enough in my mind to be able to drink, although he also said I should be strong enough to realise that it didn't actually do anything for me. Whatever his good intentions, I do think he was overestimating my strength of mind. However much I told him, he couldn't accept that I wasn't the kind of fella who could go out for a night, wake up next morning and say, Do I really want that kind of stuff? No I don't. Once I've started, I just want to go on and on. I've never been one of those balanced people who can sit in the middle of a social gathering and enjoy a couple of drinks. I've tried the controlled drinking and controlled nights out and it doesn't work for me.

So I realised the only solution was to return to NA. And as I write this I am four months clean – the second-largest amount of clean time I've done. I know you've heard this before, but hopefully something has changed this time, and I will be able to maintain it. What's more, this time I've even given up smoking cigarettes. Unbelievable, never thought I'd manage that, but I'm doing fine without the tabs.

I've been on a massive fitness drive over the past

four months and have really enjoyed it. It's a neces-
sity, actually. Not only does exercise give you your
own natural drug, it also helps fill in the time because
when you stop abusing your body you find that you
have a hell of a lot of time on your hands: a lot of
time to indulge your feelings and emotions, which
can be a bit dangerous for me. I'm not the kind of
person who can sit down and be relaxed and think,
How serene I am, isn't the world a wonderful place?
I've got to be doing things. I want to punish myself,
put my body through some sort of strenuous exercise
or go into an army camp for two months. I've never
done it, but it really does appeal to me: you know,
Live life tough. Perhaps that need to hammer yourself
in one way or another is quite sick, but I've just got
to accept that that is the way I am. Actually, the way
I am at the moment, I quite like myself.

The people at the rooms have been supportive
since I went back. I go to two or three meetings a
week. Three would probably be enough for me, but
sometimes I don't make three and feel the worse
for it. Three meetings a week keeps me grounded,
reminds me where I've come from and where I could
end up, because I see people who have just come off
a bender. And it reminds me how I can fall. Now I
don't think of myself as missing out on drink and
drugs, I just think of the misery I was left in the last
time, sitting there miserable and lonely at Sheffield.
I was so depressed I didn't want to be around anyone,
and no one wanted to be around me. Fortunately, I
realised I'd got to the point where I had to make a

choice: carry on destroying myself, spend all my time in the house with loads of people who'd do anything I wanted them to do, or get back to the rooms, which kept me in balance with myself. I realised that I'd had more times when I'd felt calm and in tune with myself when I was in the meetings; I've tried everything else and this is what works best for me.

Predictably, a year couldn't pass without me making the front pages of the newspapers, but I've got to admit this story surprised even me. 'Ronnie O'Sullivan converts to Islam', screamed the tabloid headlines. One paper even had a picture of me holding a Koran in my hand, looking way out of it. As usual, there was some truth in it, but there was also plenty that wasn't true. I suppose I've spent much of my adult life looking for different belief systems, and trying them out. In recent years I've looked into Christianity and Buddhism, and one night I was talking to my mate Naz, the boxer Prince Naseem, about Islam, and we had a long and interesting conversation. I loved the way that religion gave him such a sense of purpose. Anyway, to cut a very long and strange story short, I ended up going down to a mosque with him and some of his friends, and taking part in a service. To be honest, I didn't have a clue what was happening, but when they told me to repeat some words after them it seemed rude not to, so I did. The upshot was that I was surrounded by hundreds of people kissing and hugging me, who seemed to think I had converted to Islam.

But it was news to me. And if I gave them that impression, I'm sorry – I certainly didn't mean to. I went home, forgot about it, and then a couple of months later these stories appeared in the news-papers. It was very strange, and to be honest quite upsetting. It left me in an awkward position. I wanted to tell the truth, but I didn't want to seem as if I was knocking anyone's religion. I thought I'd just let it die down, but more and more stories were appearing, and there were all these quotes floating about saying snooker players were having a laugh about Ronnie's latest conversion, but anything that helps him find peace is good with them, that kind of thing. In the end, I decided to put out a statement to clear the air, and explain that I had plenty of Muslim friends and had attended a mosque with them, but no, I wasn't a Muslim myself. At least, not intentionally.

I'm open to all spiritual teachings. I suppose I'm just a curious sort of fella. A lot of my Muslim friends seem very happy, and I said to them I wanted to know a little bit more about it. And because they love what they do so much, they wanted me to have what they had. But I'm not ready to convert and lead my life in a Muslim way. I recently said to a newspaper that I may be ready in ten years' time, but thinking about it now, I doubt if I ever will be. I've got sex shops and own a knickers shop, I have sex with my girlfriend while we're not married, so there's no way I could live a good Muslim life.

I thought it was a wind-up when I first saw it in the newspapers, and didn't really have a clue about the consequences. But then the media started hounding me, people started telling me what a big thing it was and I remembered somebody telling me never to get involved in politics or religion; and now I know why. I'm very much a live-and-let-live person, and although I'm interested in all different spiritual practices, I could never see myself becoming a devout follower of one religion. To me, it doesn't matter what religion anybody is so long as their heart's in the right place. I think the nearest thing I've got to a religion is the NA. That's given me my own faith. There's no tough set of rules, and it's very forgiving, but I'm happy with the progress I've made, whether it's through meditation, going to meetings or going to the gym.

So it's been a roller-coaster of a year. But then again, probably not as much of a roller-coaster as previous years. Even though I have a go at myself for lack of consistency, I still won three tournaments.

The book has been brilliant for me. So many people have read it and said that they identified with me and my struggles. My dad was made up with it. He read it in one go, and told me he was going back this afternoon to read it again. He said that he wasn't just saying it because I was his son, but it was one of the best books he'd ever read. Not so sure about that one. Perhaps Dad hasn't read that many books. He told me he'd read John McEnroe's book and he thought I was like McEnroe: 'When you're snooker's good, you're up,' he said, 'and when your snooker's bad, you're down.' Apparently, McEnroe didn't want to talk to people when his tennis was bad; he used to love the practice but he'd get to competitions and think, 'Ouch, I don't like this much', and that's how I feel at times – loving the practice and build-up and then finding it all such a let-down. I don't know why, maybe it's because it's all over too quick, or because we have too high expectations for ourselves, and don't allow ourselves to enjoy the actual playing. Or perhaps I'm so busy telling myself I must win that I'm not free enough to enjoy the game.

The book also caused some controversy. Mark Williams told the press that he was angry about how he was portrayed in the book, and that I was an idiot. Likewise Stephen Hendry was annoyed. Neither of them have spoken to me for ages. The strange thing is, I thought I'd been quite complimentary to them. Yes, I'd been honest about them, but it was never my intention to attack them for the sake of it, and if they look closely enough they'll both find plenty of praise for them there. I've got to the stage of my life where I don't get bitter or hurt about others doing well at snooker. I'm content with myself, so I'm not look-ing outside of myself to find happiness, I certainly won't find happiness by willing other players to do badly. This year, in spite of what I said earlier about watching tournaments I've been knocked out of, I actually watched the World final. Four years ago I wouldn't have been able to do that, but this year I saw Williams and Doherty battling it out in the final sessions and it was some of the best snooker I've ever seen, considering the amount of pressure both of them must have been under and the lead that Williams had. Admittedly, I would have liked Ken to win, but well done to Mark. He was the best player over the seventeen days, and deserved to win. He's probably the best snooker player in the world today, end of story. On a personal level, we don't get on, but we're both big enough and ugly enough to cope with that, so good luck to him.

I've come a long way in my life over the past three or four years, and I like the journey I'm on. Hopefully, snooker can continue to be a part of that because I do love the game, and I love competing, but there are also lots of other things in my life. At the moment, I expect to spend the next ten years playing snooker. But that's today. Perhaps tomorrow I'll want to give it all up for golf or business. The shops are doing well: I'm really pleased with Viva La Diva, our upmarket sexy underwear shop on Old Compton Street in the heart of Soho. I suppose I'd never have to work again if I didn't want to, but the fact is I do. I need to keep my juices flowing. I'm trying to take things slowly, and my sobriety has got priority over everything else at the moment.

Happiness is something I've been looking for a long time, and I feel I'm as close to finding it as I ever have been. I've got a great life – going down the gym for my training, having a bit of a social life, practising my snooker and going to my little meetings – and it doesn't really get any better than that for me.

INDEX